Xponential Growth

Xponential Growth
Copyright © 2018 Mike Mastroyiannis
All Rights Reserved

ISBN-13: 978-1726353458
ISBN-10: 1726353451

All rights reserved. No part of this book may be reproduced, distributed or transmitted in any form by any means, including photocopying, recording, or by any information storage or retrieval system without prior written permission of the author, except in the case of brief quotations embodied in critical reviews and certain noncommercial uses permitted by copyright law.

Printed in the United States of America

Legal Disclaimer
The publisher and author make no representations or warranties with respect to the accuracy or completeness of the contents of this work and specifically disclaim all warranties, including, without limitation, warranties for a particular purpose. No warranty may be created or extended by sales or promotional materials. The advice and strategies contained herein are provided by the author, an expert on the subject, and may not be suitable for every situation. Neither the publisher nor the author shall be liable for damages arising here from. The fact that an organization or website is cited and/or may be a potential source of further information does not mean that the author or the publisher endorses the information that may be provided.

XPONENTIAL GROWTH

MIKE MASTROYIANNIS

Dedication

To three amazing ladies, in the sequence they entered and enriched my life:

Nadia, Alexia and Phyllis

Contents

Acknowledgments 1

Prologue / Preface 3

Chapter 1: What is changing in the 21st Century?—Innovation 7

    1.1 Linear versus Xponential 9

    1.2 The Five Mega Trends 14

    1.3 Key impacts of the Xponential technologies 33

    1.4 Innovation in the 21st Century 46

    1.5 Summary 53

Chapter 2: Understand the current business 57

    2.1 Identify and plot the key factors of competition of the industry. 59

    2.2 Draw your own company strategic map 61

    2.3 Compare the strategic maps, discuss with team and draw your conclusions 62

    2.4 Summary and deliverables 66

Chapter 3: Find out pathways to grow 67

    3.1 Identify the pain points or blocks across the customer experience cycle 75

    3.2 Find out if these pain points or blocks limit any customers or potential customers 77

    3.3 Find out after elimination of pain points which new customer groups could attract 78

3.4 Decide what pain points to eliminate and which customer and potential customer group(s) to focus 81

3.5 Understand better innovation in the Xponential 21st Century 83

3.6 Innovation in the future/Xponential culture/how to generate new concepts 96

3.7 Identify new value creations and cost reductions by analysing the eight pathways 98

3.8 Summary and deliverables........................... 114

Chapter 4: Create Xponential growth strategy per pathway 117

4.1 Analyze comments, extract insights and align in the team per pathway 126

4.2 Decide which factors of competition to eliminate, reduce, increase or create per pathway................ 127

4.3 Create the new strategic map for the specific pathway... 132

4.4 Evaluate and explain the economic benefits - repeat for the selected pathways 135

4.5 Xponential Growth 137

4.6 Summary and deliverables........................... 145

Chapter 5: Choose the best pathway(s), execute and review. 147

5.1 Evaluation process and management decision . 147

5.2 Communicate the decision internally and go for a quick market research test 151

5.3 Setup an execution team, start implementation and review results... 151

5.4 Summary and deliverables 158
Epilogue.. 159
Exhibits.. 161
Exhibit 1: Xponential Culture Matrix – 25 questions to generate new ideas and concepts....................... 161
Exhibit 2: Innovation in the future – Questions 163
About the Author 165

Acknowledgments

I would like to thank all colleagues in TenX2 for their support, suggestions and reviews.

REVIEWS

"Mike offers with Xponential Growth great insights and practical tools how to step up your game exponentially."

- **Bas Fransen**, former VP IBM and currently serial entrepreneur.

"Mike offers the most up-to-date and comprehensive understanding of the current business and technological environment and provides thought leadership on practical approaches for enterprises and start-ups in scaling stage to accelerate their growth."

- **Yip Yew Seng**, Current President of INCOSE Singapore Chapter, a global professional society in systems engineering.

Prologue / Preface

This book takes its inspiration from the potential that the Xponential 21st Century offers to any company that wants to grow their business faster. Namely, it is applicable for:

1. Established companies that need to make a shift from past business practices and successfully embrace innovation, Xponential growth, and in general, the potential of the 21st Century;
2. Start-ups that are struggling to scale their business and need inspiration and strategy to scale faster;
3. Anyone who is interested in learning about how to grow a business faster or create Xponential growth in the 21st Century.

Xponential Growth is full of inspiring, real-world examples of what is changing in the 21st Century, how leaders have disrupted industries or created totally new markets and/or expanded boundaries of industries. Xponential Growth guides you step-by-step to create Xponential growth for your company. What you will learn in this book:

- Why we live in times of Xponential growth;
- What is the mindset of growth and abundance and Why it is possible to achieve improvement and/or

growth of 10X or more instead of just 10% or 30%;
- How to leverage technologies that are already growing Xponentially to create Xponentially-growing businesses or become Xponentially more efficient;
- How to design digital business models enabling Xponential growth;
- How to find and implement new pathways of growth, resulting in Xponential growth.

After a 30-year career in innovation and leadership roles with multinational corporations and start-ups in various stages (founding, incubating and scaling), the subject of growth has always been part of my life, especially the subject of how to reduce/avoid human capacity/energy being wasted and failing to create growth—which is the norm in both the corporate and start-up worlds—and instead, generate growth. This book is the result of my own experiences with innovation, leadership, growing of businesses and start-ups, restructuring, coaching, consulting various businesses, and reading numerous books, as well as writing articles and conducting workshops.

This book explains why and what is happening in innovation in the 21st Century, how to analyse existing businesses, which innovation approaches to use, how to find pathways/options to grow, and finally, decide which pathways to use and how to execute them to create exponential growth. Oftentimes, asking the right questions is essential for success, and this book has a wealth of questions to support your growth. It includes a lot of examples to understand the "how-to," and it follows a step-by-step approach to apply it to your business!

Wishing you a lot of success in your journey with innovation and Xponential growth.

www.TenX2.com

Mike Mastroyiannis
Hong Kong, August 2018

Chapter 1: What is changing in the 21st Century?—Innovation

If we evaluate what has happened in the world of innovation the last 120 years, change is the norm and change is accelerating. The Figure 1 on the following page explains the past, the present and the future in one picture and a few words.

120 Years of Innovation and the Future Exponential Innovation- Figure 1

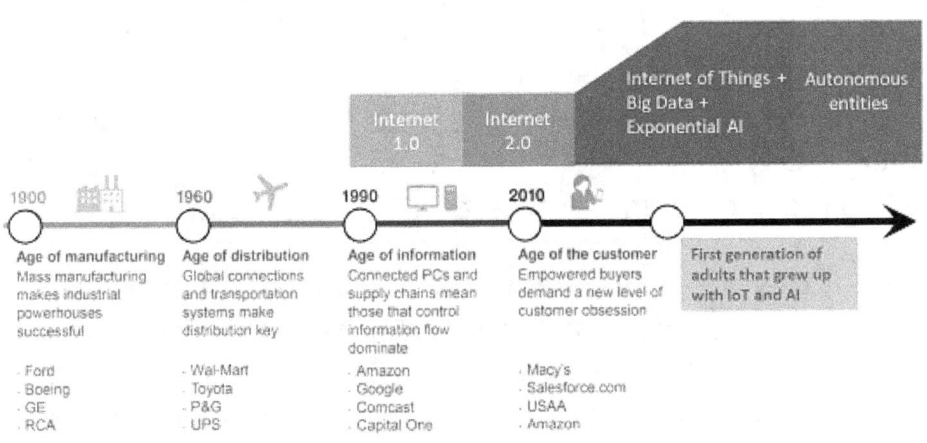

We moved from the era of *manufacturing*, to the era of *distribution*, then to the *information* era; and with the transparency and connectivity that the Internet brought us, we are now in the *customer* era. We are now moving to the era of IoT/AI, which will be followed by the era of the *autonomous entities*.

I started my career in the 80s, where globalisation was growing fast, the power had moved to distribution, the pace of doing business was relatively slow and the first personal computers started to appear. Then we moved to the information era, when computers, as well as the Internet and mobile phones, increased connectivity, resulting in faster changes and increasing the speed of doing business.

The emergence of digitalisation brought a lot of changes resulting in bankruptcies, reengineering and reorganisations or transformations of many large corporations that could not compete successfully. This lasted for almost two decades, and although digitalisation and disruption are common words in the current era, this has started in the 20th Century with industries like consumer electronics. During the 1st decade of the 21st Century, the transparency that the Internet brought increased the power of customers and consumers, enabling the dawn of the era of the customer.

Over the last 30 years, through living in various countries as well as travelling around the world, I experienced these changes, and I feel that in the 2nd decade of the 21st Century that software content is increasing dramatically. The changes enabled by new technologies like AI, Cloud computing, IoT and Robotics is not only faster, it is Xponential. The coming generation will be the first generation of adults to have grown up with IoT and AI when the acceleration of innovation and change will continue to be Xponential. As the understanding of what is changing in the 21st

Century is crucial for success, I devote proportionally more time in this chapter.

Now we start with the 1st step of our Xponential growth journey, an "outside-in" view from the perspective of any company and individual by exploring **What** is changing in the 21st Century: Innovation, see Figure 2, starting with the linear versus Xponential mindset.

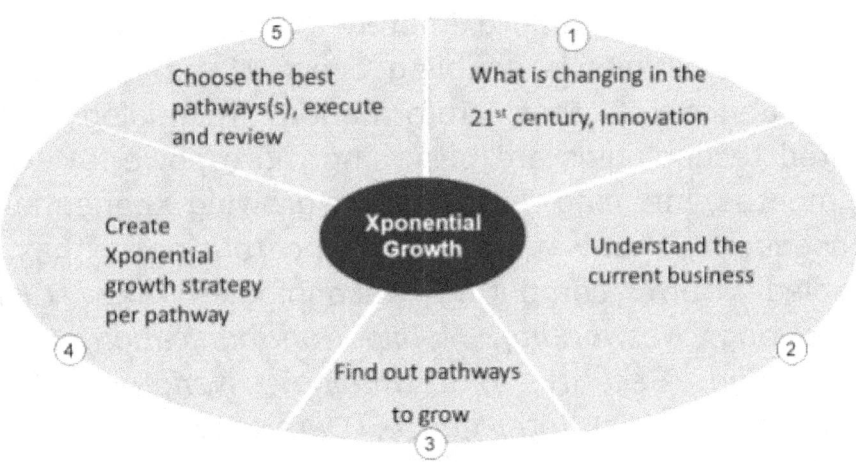

Figure 2

1.1 Linear versus Xponential

We think linearly. In fact, our brains are hardwired for linear thinking. We speculate where things will be in the future by looking back at the past. One thousand years ago, only monarchies or religions created major changes, and one hundred years ago, the industrialists and inventors (Carnegie, Edison, Rockefeller) controlled change.

In recent times, it has become possible for individuals like Jeff Bezos, Elon Musk and many other entrepreneurs, as well as initially smaller companies (such as SpaceX versus NASA and Netflix versus the cable industry) to initiate change that previously only governments or multinationals could do and in much less time.

As captured in Moore's Law, innovation with integrated circuits is doubling approximately every 18 months (the number of circuits is doubling every 18 months). As a consequence of that, Information Technology (IT) related technologies are becoming more powerful every 18 months, meaning that they are growing Xponentially. Consequently, any field of science/business that is enabled from computing technologies like *Cloud Computing, Networking, Mobile Communication, Social Networking, Security, Biotechnology, Nanotechnology, Robotics, Artificial Intelligence, Data Analytics* and *3D Printing,* is growing or becoming Xponentially more efficient. In simpler words, as a direct result of following Moore's law, all the above technologies or related business sectors are doubling in power/innovation approximately every 18 months.

Xponential technologies are driving the growth of:

- Robotics: Self driving cars and drones;
- Artificial Intelligence: Watson (IBM Computer) beats any human opponent ;
- VR/AR: DIY skills clinics;
- Cloud Computing: Cost per hour is declining monthly;

- 3D Printing: Customised cars, human body parts, modular housing etc.
- Biotechnology: Synthetic substances for fuel, food, vaccines, genes;
- Nanotechnology: Genetically modified silk is stronger than steel, graphene;
- Transformation from product economy to service and experience economy;
- IoT: Is driving efficiency in operations, preventive healthcare, maintenance and smart cities, to name a few.

To explain the effect of Xponential technologies versus linear, see Figure 3 below.

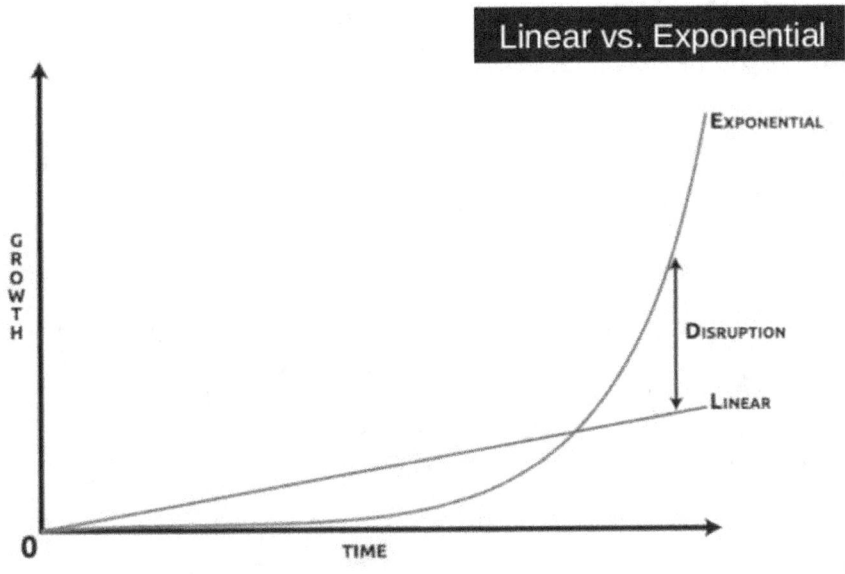

Figure 3

Any product that is digitised (e.g. images, communication, biotechnology, payments, contracts with Blockchain technology) becomes an information product and it follows the Xponential growth curve based on Moore's Law. Anything digitised can be delivered almost without cost, or at most, very low incremental cost after it has been created, resulting in high demand, and consequently, Xponential growth. Initially, the Xponential curve is slower than the linear one (see Figure 3). After the Xponential curve crosses the linear, it is already too late for the company that follows the linear curve, as it is very difficult at this point in time to catch up to the steep growth of the Xponential curve.

But how does the new technologies' lifecycle curve actually work? It is not as smooth as you might imagine, as growth for new technologies generally takes time before becoming mainstream, as shown by the Gartner Hype Cycle. See Figure 4 and the explanation that follows below.

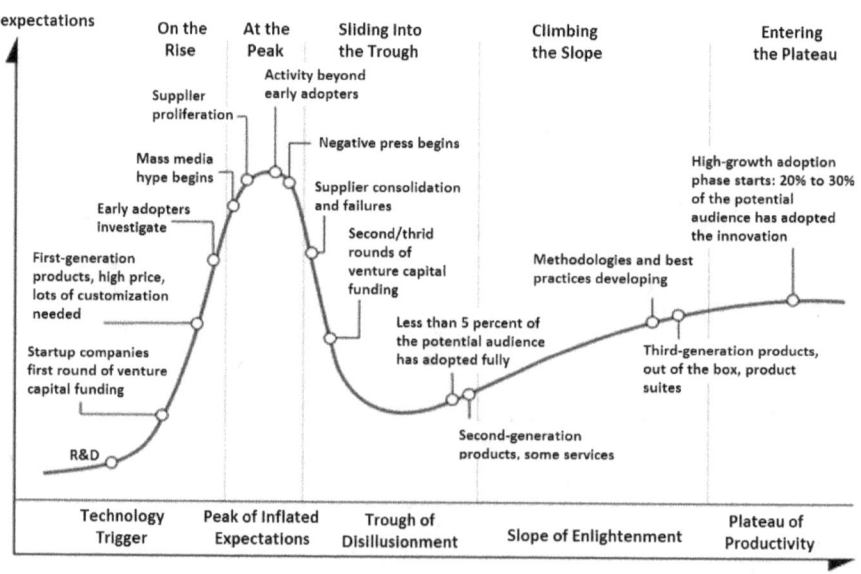

Figure 4, Gartner Hype Cycle

In general, we overestimate the technological capabilities in the short term and underestimate what they can do in the long term. As all of the new technologies described above follow these five stages of the Gartner Curve, it is imperative that they are be understood by everyone involved in any innovation.

1. Technology trigger

At this stage, start-ups raise their first rounds of capital; they create the first stage of new technologies; they see many applications and opportunities with few of the downsides, and first/early adopters evaluate the technologies/products. During this stage we see the 1st growth of the technology, which is not yet sustainable.

2. Peak of inflated expectations

Mass media hype starts with inflated expectations, where imagination outpaces reality. Many companies enter the ecosystem at this stage and later on, negative press begins.

3. Trough of disillusionment

During this stage, the inflated expectations begin to die down and negative press is increasing; people talk negatively about the technology, even if the technology continues to grow. The 2nd and 3rd rounds of VC investment are taking place, still with low adoption.

4. Slope of enlightenment

The technology is growing Xponentially; the 3rd and 4th generations of products are appearing with rapid advancements that surpass expectations. This is the 2nd Xponential growth of the technology, which is sustainable.

5. Plateau of productivity

Growth starts to slow down; 20-30% of the potential customers have adopted the product; a lot of revenue is generated; and people start to take the technology and products for granted.

After this brief introduction about Xponential growth, we are going to switch to a discussion about what is changing in the 21st Century, starting with the five Megatrends. There are more megatrends than just these five, but according to the author, these are the most important for the purpose of growth.

1.2 The Five Mega Trends

In order to understand better the major changes taking place in the 21st Century we need first to understand what are the world megatrends:

1. *Acceleration of urbanisation*
2. *An aging world*
3. *Greater global connections*
4. *Climate change*
5. *Accelerating technological change*

We will now describe these trends with more focus on **accelerating technological change**, as it will have a major impact on the world in the decades to come.

1.2.1 Acceleration of Urbanisation

Countries are becoming more urbanised than ever, with 65 million people moving from rural areas to cities every year, according to the McKinsey Global Institute. In the past 20 years, global economic growth has lifted approximately 650 million people from poverty, with 50% of these living in China. The great majority of these people, particularly in Asia and more specifically, China, moved to cities. By 2025, 50% of the world's urban population will be in Asia, with 2.5 billion people living in Asian cities. This is a truly Asian Century.

By 2030, 6 out of 10 people will live in cities (7 out of 10 by 2050) with a 150% increase in consumption from 2010 to 2030, especially in emerging markets. This is from 12 trillion USD to 30 Trillion USD.

Concentration of population historically leads to a spurt in ideas and innovation! This has been observed since people started meeting in coffee shops in the 17th and 18th Century.

1.2.2 An ageing world

Healthcare is one of the least Internet connected industries, together with education and government. Traditional healthcare with inefficient hospitals, administration and insurance is ready for disruption. Healthcare is continuing to shift toward consumer driven, value-based care, with opportunities for technological solutions. Many companies work with mobile solutions on monitoring, cost competitiveness and disease prevention. Below you will find examples of the changes that have happened in healthcare so far, and we are still in the early stages of growth:

Biotechnology became digital. DNA sequencing went from from 10000000 USD in 2007 to 200 USD in 2017, a reduction of 50000 times in 10 years; synthetic substances are being used for fuel, food, vaccines and soon genes! Stem cells will extend human life to over 150 years.

- The genome is digitised.
- Remote diagnosis is digitised.
- Smart Algorithms look for disease patterns.
- Smart Algorithms look for diseased cells (breast tumour cells).
- DNA-based preventive medicine and personalised remedies are being used.
- Organs can be recreated and updated.
- Augmented living: we are able to live longer and better.

1.2.3 Greater global connectivity

The greater global connectivity impacts, mainly positively, many aspects of the economy, including the way we live, work and interact with others. These are the major impacts:

- Getting what you want when you want (food, transportation, education, communication);
- Continuous e-commerce and global trading growth;
- Enabling flexible labour and shared economy with improved efficiency;

- Changing the nature and location of work for millions to home offices;
- Benefiting and empowering consumers;
- Optimising the customer experience;
- Internet of everything just around the corner: Sensors, communication technologies and apps will drive this. Data mining will shape this (app Annie), further augmenting our intelligence, and finally, all of the above will result in massive data-driven digital businesses growth;
- Has some adverse effects on the attention span and health of humans;
- Projects from Google (balloons, called project Loon), Facebook (solar drones) and various satellite projects from other innovative companies aim to hyper connect the world, adding billions to the net.

Figure 5 on the following page shows the optimisation of the customer experience, where the advances in connectivity and other technologies enable delivery of the right message at the right time to the right person. Alibaba in China uses three enablers to achieve the following:

- Market place platform with billions of transactions per month;
- Best insights to consumer behaviour; and
- Deep technological capabilities.

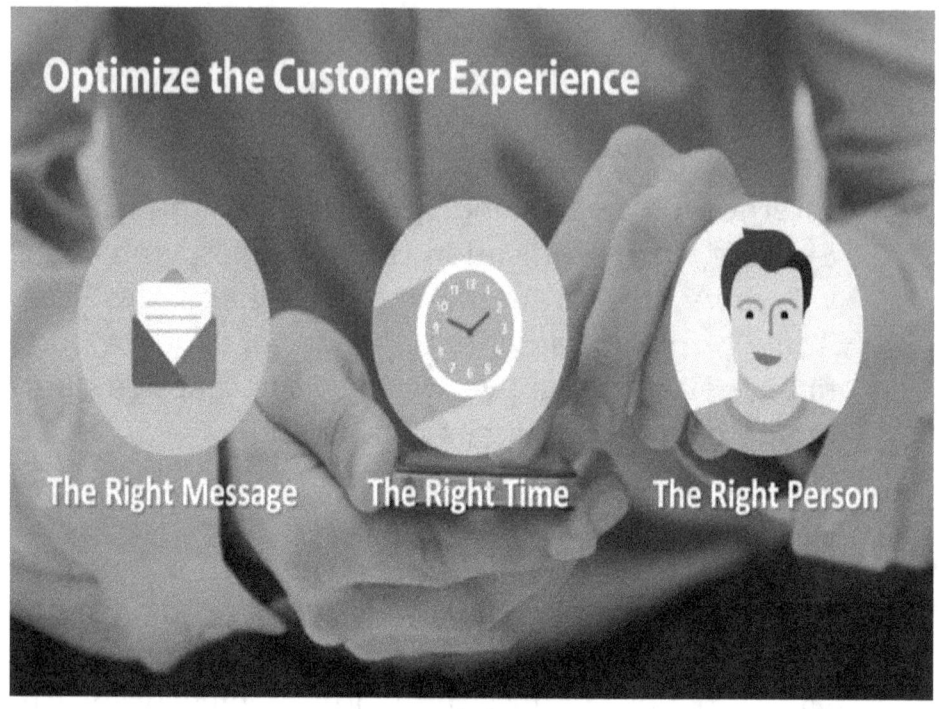

Figure 5

Figure 6 shows the massive growth of data, especially cloud data.

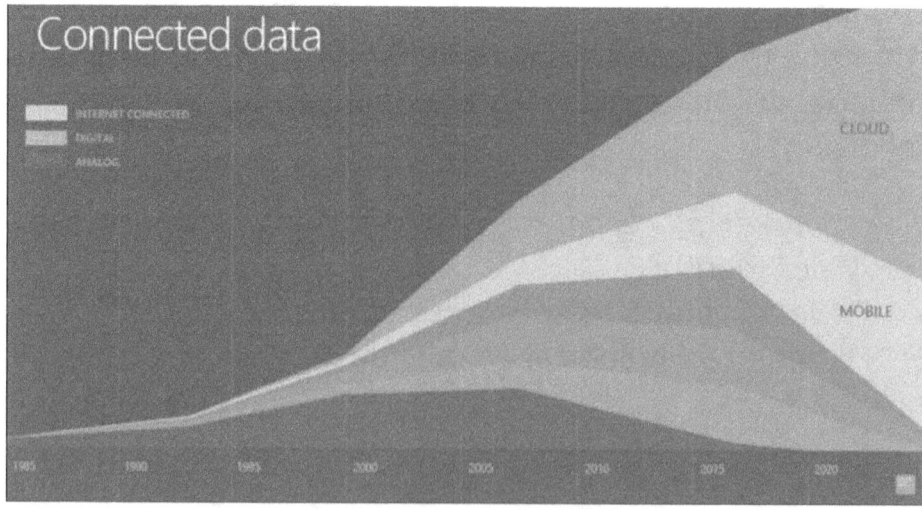

Figure 6

1.2.4 Climate change

This is an opportunity for accelerating innovation and growth. The impact on innovation stemming from climate change is regarded as potentially disruptive by industry leaders: 46% Utilities sector, 36 % Communications sector and 33% Infrastructure sector. Climate change is both a threat and an opportunity for the private sector:

- After Paris COP 21, developing countries will need $100 Billion/year of new investments over the next 40 years in order to build resilience.
- Mitigation costs are expected to be in the range of $140-$175 Billion/year by 2030.
- This enormous burden will need the buy-in and participation of the private sector.

But why should businesses, whose main responsibility is to their shareholders, need to care about climate change? A study by CitiGroup found that rampant warming could shave up to $72 trillion off the world's gross domestic product, while another report in the journal, Nature found it could reduce average global incomes by nearly a quarter.

From Harvard Business Review: *"Climate change threatens our supply chain, our customers' businesses, and the communities we're part of. If we want to stay in business for the long term, contributing to the fight against climate change is just smart strategy."* Dean Scarborough, CEO of Avery Dennison

What needs to be mentioned is that growth in urbanisation and consumption leads to increase in pollution and adverse effects for the environment if no special measures are taken to create sustainable growth. The belt and road initiative of China (BRI), probably the biggest infrastructure project of the 21st Century, is involving more than 3 billion people as well as a vast territory of emerging countries that need infrastructure investments/projects to grow. To avoid any further environmental damage, we need to take drastic measures to implement these projects in an environmentally sustainable way. China, the biggest polluter so far in the 21st Century, is making a lot of corrective actions in their own environmental projects. For example, the world's biggest floating solar power plant is in China; there has been a massive deployment of solar farms across the country; it is the world leader in electric busses, cars, bikes and more. The hope is that the same effort and discipline will be shown in the BRI infrastructure projects.

1.2.5 Accelerating technological change
With information technology growing Xponentially, every field of science/business that is enabled by computing technologies is either growing or will become Xponentially more efficient. It took radio 38 years to have 50 million listeners, TV 13 years, the Internet only 3 years and Facebook only 1 year. In the past, the product adoption (S) curve was decades long, but nowadays, we talk only about years. Let's now describe in more detail a few technologies and applications that are accelerating Xponentially.

The essence of any technological innovation is about the value it brings to customers.

1. Computing power and cloud

Moore's Law is still in full effect. Computing technologies are doubling in performance almost every 18 months on average and are creating Xponential growth for all IT-related industries. (If something doubles 10X, it becomes 1000—1024 to be accurate—and if something doubles 20X, it becomes a million.) The Xponential growth will not stop and it will continue with Quantum Computing.

The growth in Integrated Circuits (IC) technology has been spectacular, with 2000-3000 transistors in 1 IC in the beginning of the 1970s, to 15 billion transistors in 2018. This is XPONENTIAL growth; everything becomes cheaper and better and faster, year after year. Cloud computing, which is becoming 10% more cost efficient every year, supports Xponential growth in everything that requires computing. Finally, based on the Xponential growth of IC technology, it is expected that a $1000 computer will be available in 2023 that uses the power of your brain.

Based on economic data, the great majority of *economic growth comes from Information Technology Industries!*

2. Data explosion and mining algorithms becoming mainstream

Data is to this Century what electricity was to the 20th Century. 300 billion emails are sent per day and terabytes of data are uploaded to Facebook, Wechat and Youtube every day. With an 80% data growth rate, imagine what will happen in the coming 10 years! AI,

IoT, autonomous vehicles and other technologies will generate huge quantities of data. What is important is to generate useful insights from these data, and this will be our major challenge together with storage. For example, App Annie is becoming more popular than Nielsen or GFK and there will be growing and smooth integration of data-mining insights into our daily lives.

3. Sensors and the Internet of Things (IoT)

Sensors are becoming cheaper and more connected. By 2020, it is expected that there will be 30-40 billion connected devices in the world.

But what is IoT? IoT is a huge network of systems consisting of sensors, devices, connectivity, data and intelligent data analytics algorithms. Although HW (hardware) has been marginalised over the last 10 years, with the IoT, which is all about systems and solutions, HW is again becoming important. In order to become successful, the IoT needs to offer value (efficiency, innovation, new business models) to the enterprise world and make life simpler, convenient or cheaper for consumers to adopt. As with social networking, where billions of people are connected, with the IoT we will expand the connections to include various devices. In fact, networks or better network power will change the world order and the IoT together with all human networks will create the *Internet of Everything*.

But what are key facts, including benefits, of the IoT?

- It will grow from 10 billion devices in 2015 to 30-40 billion in 2020.
- IoT aims to make business operations more efficient and make life simpler, more convenient or cheaper for consumers to adopt.
- It will enable faster Innovation cycles.
- It will drive cost reductions.
- It supports the shift from products to services (e.g. shared cars, construction tools as a service).
- It enables new business models, especially with real time data insights.
- It rides on the power of cloud and mobile technologies.
- It is enabled from sensor, communication, security, data analytics and Artificial Intelligence technologies.
- It facilitates the expansion of markets: From car to mobility.

What are the key markets for the IoT?

- Health care: Remote health diagnostics with body sensors to detect diseases, feedback for fitness improvement;
- Smart Cities/Transportation: Efficiency in infrastructure usage, UBER network;
- Energy Efficiency/ Building Automation;
- Quality of key products: Monitoring of key components e.g. airplane turbines;
- Insurance premiums and banking loans: Variable pricing based on health condition (fitness level) and driving behaviour;

- Retail: Checkout-less shopping, location advertisement in-store with superb customer experiences;
- Consumer: control of various household devices through a single app or voice control;
- Manufacturing: Automation with robots; and
- Agriculture: Improve productivity using drones and sensors.

As there are so many benefits, why doesn't this industry grow faster? The issue is that there are a few enablers that are missing; or, in fact, there are a few barriers for adoption. For simpler systems it is already possible, and here we talk about bigger networks. But what are the barriers against adoption of the IoT?

- Technology complexity;
- Lack of interoperability standards that are slowly emerging (e.g. Lora);
- Security;
- Low power consumption to enable longevity (10 - 20 years), otherwise, the maintenance expenses make the ROI too low, if not negative;
- Privacy and location of data is another challenge.

4. *Mobile, wireless 5G, e-commerce, online* and social platforms

With 3.6 billion connected (49% Internet penetration in 2017) and another 2 billion people joining the connected world in the next 5-7 years, economic growth as well as innovation is expected to skyrocket. But how will the new entrants reshape innovation and economy? Companies that will focus to serve the new entrants, even if they have low purchasing power, will benefit a lot due to the big size of additional online population.

With mobile devices, people are used to being online 24/7 and getting what they want when they want! In China alone, there are 600 million people using mobile payments (Wechat and Alipay), while in 2017 the online payments reached 16 trillion RMB. The online sales in China exceed 20% as a percentage of retail sales, whilst in the USA it is just a bit more than 12%. The ease of mobile payments with Wechat and Alipay is supporting tremendous growth of online sales. The top 20 internet technology companies are from the USA and China: 11 from the USA and 9 from China. If we compare 4 of these, we observe the following:

Amazon versus **Alibaba**:

- While Amazon is 5x bigger in sales than Alibaba, Alibaba has 3x bigger GMV (Gross merchandise volume).
- While Amazon has 31% revenue from outside of the USA as a percentage of sales, Alibaba has only 8%.
- Alibaba has 3X the free cash flow of Amazon.
- Alibaba has a much higher gross margin.
- Alibaba has acquired many companies from other Asian countries.
- Both have mobile payment platforms (with Alibaba having more users), digital entertainment business, physical retail and strong cloud platforms, with Amazon the market leader.

Facebook versus **Tencent**:

- Facebook has more than double the users of Tencent (more than 2 billion versus 1 billion).
- While Tencent has multiple revenue streams (games, payments, e-commerce commissions, ads and more), Facebook is mainly dependent on ads and started with e-commerce.
- Tencent has a powerful payment platform, with more than 400 million using it.
- Facebook is global (except China), while Tencent is mainly in China and just starting to have international ambitions.

This high e-commerce growth, access to a lot of content and knowledge, with our activities mainly driven by apps or software, being no longer hardware confined is augmenting our intelligence in preparation for more artificial intelligence. Smartphones have become the remote controls of our lives. See Figure 7.

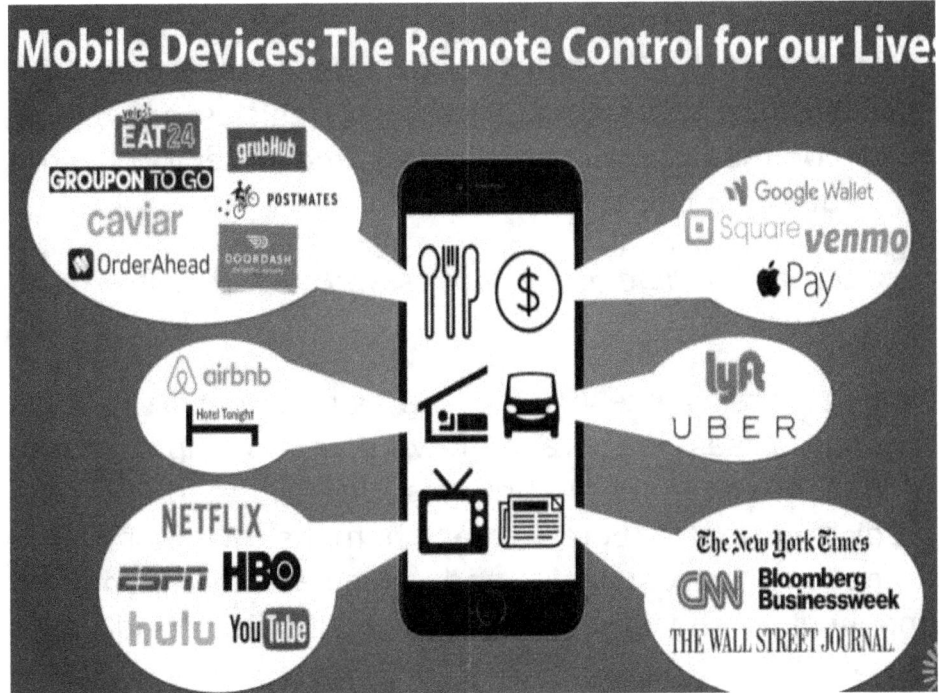

Figure 7

Another major technological innovation that will create major impact from 2020/2021 onwards is 5G, the next generation of wireless network. A semi-agreed standard, it is touted that it will change the world, but there will be some challenges as it operates within a higher GHz frequency spectrum than 4G with a few things that are of major importance:

- The high speed of 5G will enable the disruption of the current wired cable television distribution model.
- Incredible speed up to 10Gbps, which is 33X faster than the fastest LTE-A version now, 300Mbps.
- Wireless providers will have more data than Facebook and Google combined.

- 5G has very low latency; 1ms is the target versus 70ms for 4G networks. Low latency is essential for various types of autonomous vehicles and drone communication, smart cities and other connected device applications.

5. *Artificial Intelligence, Robotics and VR/AR just around the corner*

Artificial intelligence (AI) will be transformative to lives and businesses. We already have many examples where AI has achieved breakthroughs. AI can read lips and predict elections better than humans; Watson (IBM Computer) saves lives and eliminates any human opponent in chess and jeopardy, while DeepMind beats the world's Go champion (see Figure 8). Google is learning from our bookings, activities and behaviour, and it reminds us about our appointments or travel. In the future, it is also expected to even make suggestions on what to do next. Amazon Echo and Google Home are an intelligent combination of AI and voice recognition that is improving daily and will make it easier to control various activities at home and beyond. Google voice recognition technology has already surpassed the threshold of human accuracy (95%).

China has a tremendous number of data, is investing heavily for innovation in AI and it is expected to take over the lead in five years. In fact, with massive government and private investments, China might be leading in image and face recognition.

For robotics, industrial robots costing $500,000 USD in 2007, cost only $10,000 USD in 2017. That's a cost reduction of 50X in 10 years. Drones that cost $100,000 USD in 2007, cost only $100 USD in 2017, showing a 1000X cost reduction in 10 years. While robots are becoming cheaper, drones have become very cheap, and many companies are experimenting with drone delivery (Amazon, 7-11), and the investments on flying cars are increasing rapidly.

But what about the practical applications of robotics now? Let's take, for example, the retail environment: As robots are a novelty, they attract people to see them in action, improve usage of vertical storage space where humans cannot easily retrieve things, help to keep track on inventory, and finally, are guiding customers on premises such as voice and image recognition, which are advancing rapidly.

For VR and AR, we are still in the initial stage of development, with bulky headsets that are hard to use beyond the early adopters. Like mobile phones that started big and bulky with miniaturisation and further improvements of various technologies like powerful processors, memory, battery density, display (e.g. OLED) and optics, we can expect slim and lightweight headsets to become integrated in our daily lives before they are integrated in our bodies.

Figure 8

6. *Nanotechnology and machine learning*

In the past, engineers discovered new materials through trial and error and in general experimentation. Today, engineers work with material discovery software to discover and design new materials for various applications. Nanotechnology is the branch of technology dealing with dimensions and tolerances of less than 100nm, especially the manipulation of individual atoms and molecules. With machine learning and the Xponential growth of computing, the trial and error has been replaced with intelligent computational methods. Currently, and especially in the near future, the material scientists will specify the desired properties of materials for specific applications, and the machine learning programs will return the optimal material composition by analysing data and solving complex quantum physics equations. Nanotechnology has already produced genetically modified silk stronger than steel and artificial/manmade diamonds. For the case of diamonds, which are too expensive when made artificially, if we extrapolate from the experience of manmade pearls, in the future the price of diamonds will decrease dramatically.

7. 3D Printing

After the mass manufacturing era, where we can serve millions of users with similar products, with 3D printing we are going to experience the next stage of evolution: mass customisation, where small series of production—or even one unique product—is economically feasible. AI/machine learning and 3D printing enables small workshops, as well as individuals, to invent, design and produce their own customised products, and finally, automated factories are increasing with the industrial IoT, AI, 3D printing farms and collaborative bots. 3D printing is already used to produce customised cars and human organs, and 3D printers are dematerialising from $40,000 USD in 2007 to $100 USD in 2017 >>> 400X cost reduction in 10 years.

8. *Block chain and digitised currencies*

Block chains are public and immutable ledgers that can be programmed to automatically collect and store information. You can effectively store any type of data, and the information is encrypted and validated in such a way that no single entity could corrupt or manipulate the system in their favour. The ledger distributes the computing power across all computer nodes in the network, mitigating the threat of hacking, as there is no central point to attack.

With the invention of block chain, new secure digital direct payments, initial coin offerings (ICO) where funds are raised for new cryptocurrency-related ventures (to bypass the rigorous and regulated capital raising process), new secure supply chain business models as well as numerous other applications (e.g. secure and smart contracts) will happen without central authority. The system is secure and can be used for many secure data transfer applications as long as there is no need for high processing speeds or a high volume of data to be transferred. As distributed systems without central authority are disruptive for the current ecosystem and require new regulations, it will take longer to be implemented. See Figure 9.

Figure 9

9. *3D Memory, DNA*

With the tremendous growth of data, the need for more memory is paramount. The good news is that in less than 30 years, the memory cost per GB went from $100 USD to almost $0.02 USD. This is a cost reduction of 5000X. 3D solid-state memory is a good first step to support the first stages of the Xponential growth of data. At the same time, even with skyrocketing investment in data storage, the capacity increase in data centres is falling behind the growth of data. The solution is first to become more selective with what we need to store and 2nd, and most importantly, to develop a new storage technology suitable for the 21st Century needs. The promising new technology is to use DNA for data storage, by encoding bits of data into tiny molecules of DNA. A few companies, including Microsoft among others, are working on the subject, and the target is to fit entire data centres in a few litres of DNA!

1.3 Key impacts of the Xponential technologies

With all these Xponential technologies growing so fast, what are the major impacts to the economy and society at large?

1.3.1 Dematerialisation:
Physical products become digitised and are distributed as bits.

As I have personal experiences with the impacts of dematerialisation, I feel strongly about it. Working for the consumer electronics industry in the A/V field, and later on with mobile communications, I felt the effects of the digitalisation with the tremendous increase of competition. Toward the end of the '90s, various consumer electronics functions started to become more and more integrated within powerful ICs, giving the opportunity for more and more companies to more easily design various digital products. In the 1st decade of the 21st Century, the power of these ICs became so strong that with a few ICs, the industry designed powerful mobile phones, other mobile digital products like music, video, digital navigation devices and later on, smart phones. By 2008/2009, with maturity, they had developed powerful wireless connectivity (3G, WiFi), and with new emerging technologies like mobile apps and crowdsourcing technologies (enabled from GPS and wireless) came the dawn and reality of multi-sided digital platform businesses like AirBnB, UBER, DIDI and MOBIKE. Without any further comments, the examples below explain well the concept of dematerialisation:

- Consumer electronics product categories (audio, camera, video, GPS) have been almost eliminated by smart phones. Hardware has been to a great extent replaced with firmware and cloud software.
- Transportation: Using UBER/DIDI instead of owning a car, as the total lifetime cost of vehicle ownership is higher.
- Books: From physical hardcopy to online books (bits), from DVD to online streaming.

1.3.2 Demonetisation: *Reduction of the value of a market segment (especially service costs) by introducing a new business model.*

When a business model changes (e.g. from paid to ad-based) for the service that has been digitised, the cost of replication or transmission is almost 0, resulting finally in demonetisation (e.g. digital communication and photography). The examples below are evidences of demonetisation in a number of market sectors:

- WhatsApp > Long distance calls
- iTunes > Record stores
- Amazon > Book stores, supermarkets
- AirBnB > Hotel chains and partly travel platforms; AirBnB has exceeded 100 million guest arrivals in 2017.
- UBER/DIDI > Car as a service, taxi fleets and more. Using UBER is already cheaper in New York, Chicago and Los Angeles versus owning a car.
- Netflix and YouTube > Have demonetised entertainment.

We expect more market segments/industries to demonetise and mention below a few more examples, including the reasons why:

- Food cost > will decrease as vertical farming will increase local production, reducing transportation and storage costs.
- Housing cost > will decrease because of 3D printing and robotics, which will demonetise the cost of building; you can work in the autonomous car, reducing the need to live downtown and/or work from home with virtual reality. This will start with smaller apartments, which are expected to be the trend in our world of high population growth.

- Education cost > is decreasing with Coursera, Khan Academy and the upcoming AI revolution.
- Healthcare costs > will decrease with diagnostics through wearables, gene sequencing, AI, robots supporting the elderly and 3D printed medicine.

Dematerialisation and *Demonetisation* are mainly the results of software content increase in any product, service, solution or experience in almost all market sectors. Please see Figure 10.

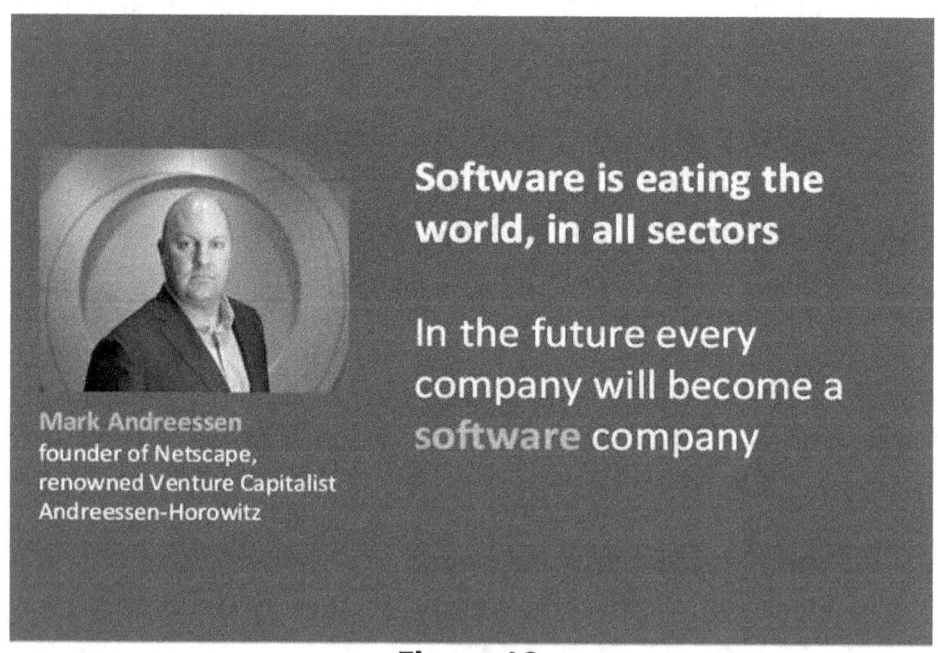

Figure 10

1.3.3 Democratisation: Availability of key technologies /applications to almost everybody. Smartphones become the platform to access everything.

The examples below explain well the concept of democratisation:

- Power of the Individual

  - Individuals with Smartphones have more power in their hands than any president of any country 20 years ago.
  - A few individuals together can build powerful companies utilising the power of the crowdsourcing and crowdfunding. For crowdsourcing and crowdfunding, see the extensive explanation in Chapter 3.
  - Individuals through social networks have tremendous influence on brands, and not just the other way around, as in the past.

- Unlimited computing power (cloud computing)
- Cheaper energy (solar and wind, 5-6 generations away to cover all earth needs?)
- Artificial Intelligence (virtual assistants, healthcare)
- Unlimited competences/cost competitive resources (crowdsourcing, crowdfunding)
- Unlimited education (free or low cost > online universities)
- Free communication (smartphones, Internet, WhatsApp, Skype) and mobile phones changed Africa by facilitating cheap/easy communication and mobile payments, resulting in faster economic growth.

1.3.4 Industry and market boundaries are fading

In the 20th Century, most of the technologies were industry-specific, making it difficult for a company to make a move to another industry. In the 21st Century, as many technologies have become more easily accessible and cross many industries, the results are massive changes in market and industry boundaries as well as new business models emerging. My personal experiences are coming from the transition from consumer electronics to lighting, energy efficiency and solutions businesses. In the 20th century, the lighting industry, excluding the luminaires market, was a capital-intensive industry with a lot of process technology involved. In this way, not many companies could enter the general lighting industry.

In the 21st Century, the introduction of digital LED technology created the opportunity for many consumer electronics manufacturers that had already felt the effects of digitalisation and could not compete anymore in consumer electronics, as well as other companies related to electronics, to enter the LED lighting market. This became possible because the new market/industry was not capital intensive and the technologies/competences involved were known or accessible to these companies. Such technologies/competences included design and manufacturing of electronics, wireless and network connectivity, systems software and speed of doing business. Below you will find examples of boundary changes from the most recent 10 years of the 21st century.

Re-definition of markets, from product-specific to customer need-centric: car market becomes mobility market, meaning that car manufacturers or other industry players, like Apple and Google, can enter the mobility market with the operating system or A/V or connectivity platform for autonomous vehicles.

The definition of an industry is changing dramatically as digital technologies create new businesses that transcend traditional industry borders (e.g. Google, Apple, Alibaba, Tencent, Amazon...). Because many of the new technologies like cloud, machine learning, data analytics and AI cross many industries, traditional core businesses can capture new value by harnessing these technologies in other industries to deliver Xponential growth.

Examples include:

- *Google:* Google is using various technologies (Mobile AI, Cloud Computing Machine Learning/AI, High Speed Internet, IoT, Biotechnology and Genetics and Crowdsourcing) that cross many industries (Education, Finance, Transportation, Entertainment, Communication, Military, Medical) to expand their activities beyond their main revenue generator (Search/Google Ads). Google creates value with Google Play (media), Android (handsets) and Google Wallet (retail) and captures value through ad sales (advertising), its core business. In fact, Google is expanding its ad platform to an e-commerce one, with the ability to order products using *Google Home*.
- *Amazon*: Creates value with Kindle (handset) and Amazon apps (media) and captures value through e-commerce, its core business. In fact, Amazon is expanding its e-commerce platform with 1-click

checkout and *Amazon Echo* to a sponsored ad platform.

1.3.5 High Scalability: At least 10X Better/ Bigger/ Faster

In the 20th Century, any design was a trade-off between cost, quality and time of completion. In the 21st Century, the power of the new technologies offers the possibility to eliminate these trade-offs. Xponential technologies are not about incremental improvement; they are about radical and huge improvements in something. Despite the fact that we are generally resistant to change, we will always continue to adopt things that are 10X better or even more. This means that solving problems that make our lives 10X better will be always in demand. Moreover, the Xponentially growing technologies allow us to make the shift to Better AND Bigger AND Faster AND Cheaper instead of the traditional Better OR Faster OR Cheaper.

The examples below explain the principle in more detail:

- Smartphones, including all functions, are better AND cheaper AND easier to use than previous phones and all devices they have replaced like IPod, camera, navigation system, or video recorder.

- WhatsApp and Wechat are cheaper AND easier to use AND offer a wider variety of functions than traditional mobile phones.

- Drones for many applications are cheaper AND faster to deploy AND easier to use: Taking pictures for big agricultural areas or for checking progress of big real estate projects versus other methods like using a helicopter or people.

- Automotive industry: In the future it is expected that autonomous vehicles used as taxis will be cheaper AND have better service AND be safer than current taxis.

- Upcoming super markets or coffee shops automated with less people and no cashiers etc. will be cheaper AND make it easier to shop AND will be faster to check out than current supermarkets.

1.3.6 Crowd-based resources on demand: *You can now hire an expert on demand, which is a win-win for both parties.*

Many companies make better use of the world's resources to become a more innovative and better performing company. Millions of individuals, including myself, crowdsource many organisational capabilities in a very competitive performance/cost ratio. In the USA only, there are 6.8 million on-demand platform workers and UBER has 3 million driver-partners worldwide:

Design (website, logo, marketing materials using platforms like Fiverr, Upwork, 99 designs), concept design ideas from communities (Kickstarter, Indiegogo), collaborative innovation/ideation (Spigit), concept validation (Reward crowdfunding e.g. Indiegogo), computer resources (Amazon, Rackspace), on demand workforce (Freelancer), prototypes (Techshop), video commercials (Tongal), incentive competitions for breakthrough solutions with data (Kaggle), virtual assistants, and finally, funding (Kickstarter, Indiegogo, Crowdfunder).

1.3.7 Bringing everything together - Smart city
We have already seen what is changing in the 21st Century, the five megatrends, and in more detail, the accelerating technological change, including its major impacts (dematerialisation, demonetisation, democratisation, market and industry change of boundaries, high scalability and crowd or community resources on demand). If there is one concept that brings it all together this is smart city, and below we describe what it is in order to give a good example of what we have described so far.

With the forecast that by 2030, 6/10 of Earth's inhabitants, and by 2050, 7/10 of Earth's inhabitants, will be living in urban areas/cities, the UN projects that by 2050, the demand for water and energy will increase by 55%. By 2035, the demand for energy will increase by 33 percent. As people migrate to cities, existing infrastructure will need to be improved or we will face significant shortages. The main aim is to address urban challenges like city management, sustainability (lower carbon emissions), efficiency in everything, safety, and finally, the most important: how efficiently a city can deliver services that its citizens actually need in order to improve their quality of life.

The good news is that with new technologies, like big data analytics generated from smart sensors, artificial intelligence, robotics, renewable energy efficient systems, intelligent lighting, 3D printing, WiFi, 5G digital communication, vertical hydroponic farming and transportation technologies (autonomous cars, flying cars, hyperloop, etc.), we can imagine new systems that are far more efficient and offer far greater performance than the ones around today. As many people talk about the future belonging to smart cities, what is the definition of a smart city?

*"Smart cities use digital information, sensing, communication and computing technologies to enhance quality and performance of urban services, to reduce costs, resource consumption and to engage more effectively and actively with its citizens in order to enhance the **quality of life**."*

To create smart cities, you need to pay attention to various areas of the economy and society at large:

- Smart Citizens first and foremost, which leads to:
- Smart Education >> Investing in education and especially in STEAM in the universities;
- Smart Healthcare >> Investing in remote healthcare monitoring;
- Smart Buildings >> Investing in energy-efficient buildings;
- Smart Energy >> Investing in renewable energy and IoT systems;
- Smart Infrastructure >> Investing in the IoT, smart lighting, image sensing, digital signage, charging points, parking and traffic monitoring;
- Smart Transportation >> Investing in autonomous vehicles, smart sensors and communication; and

- Smart Communication >> Investing in 5G and low power, wide-area networks

The good news is that we have almost all the technologies to enable things that were impossible 20 or even 10 years ago, and it will be a different approach for new cities and already established ones. For established ones, the needs of a cold city in the winter, like Beijing or Moscow (snow and central heating is part of daily life for months) are different than a warmer climate city like Hong Kong, or a tropical climate city like Singapore. In fact, the biggest challenge of an established city is the lack of foundational infrastructure/standards for the IoT and other communication. For new smart cities it is less challenging, and we already know that the most efficient cities are the ones that bring people to the centre of the smart city, combining residences, work areas, hospitality/entertainment venues and public utilities within the same area. But if we have the technologies to create smart cities, what is key to making this reality faster?

Start with the highest value creation for improvement of services/quality of life, not only infrastructure.

As the challenge is not really technological, what are the key enablers to create results faster?

- *Government leadership with bold targets.* Cities like Dubai and Singapore give the example with their five-year plans of where they want to be, e.g Dubai has set targets for 2021 for 3D printing, automated transportation trips, the number of smart and solar powered street lighting, free WiFi and digital signage.

- *Create awareness among citizens and focus on education toward smart citizens.* Invest in high-school and university education, e.g. focus on STEAM. This is obvious as when citizens are aware and educated about the subject, they will not only be supportive, but will participate and contribute with ideas toward a smarter city. Focus on education to embrace the mindset of experimentation, seeing failure as learning, and thinking big.

- *Enable and stimulate collaboration among all parties:* Government organisations, established companies, start-ups and citizens. This is the biggest obstacle, as many times governments and private organisations have different interests (economic, societal), mindsets, and finally, behaviour. Stimulate collaboration of established companies with start-ups, as there are more new ideas generated from the start-up ecosystem than established companies. Finally, start implement-tation with a new neighbourhood like many other smart cities around the world.

- *Sharing of data/insights among cities and organisations.* Learn from other cities instead of reinventing the wheel.

- *Sharing of data for free to attract start-ups and established companies to invest in the city to create new applications.* Create regulations to enable sharing of data/insights among various organisations to speed up knowledge building (e.g. mobility and transportation data).

In summary, to become successful with creating a smart city, every city needs to have a vision of the future and alignment among growth drivers, quality of life and connected/smart city objectives. Bold objectives, education of citizens, collaboration among all parties involved and smart sharing of data/insights will achieve results.

1.4 Innovation in the 21st Century

As many 21st Century technologies are growing Xponentially, with growing urbanisation and greater advances in connectivity and transparency enabled by the Internet, the innovation rate is accelerating. In order to be successful with innovation in the 21st Century, new approaches are necessary. In this part, there is a short introduction about the new innovation principles for the 21st Century as well as a few powerful practical innovation methods. More depth about innovation will be given in Chapter 3. But what are the new principles that will determine the success of innovation?

1. *Create a transformative purpose, embrace autonomy and speed*

Why?

A transformative purpose attracts talent, creates a community around and enables you to compete better. It is transformational in the sense that it inspires employees and other stakeholders to do great work.

According to new university research, both in the USA and the UK, the 21st Century motivators are Purpose, Autonomy and Mastery, and there is a need for a higher aspirational purpose that captures the hearts and minds of those inside and outside of the organisation. The link https://youtu.be/rrkrvAUbU9Y is an excellent video explaining the above mentioned 21st Century motivators. The greater connectivity and the new technologies allow for unprecedented speed of access and decision-making and that is why there is need for more autonomy and less or no hierarchy.

2. *Create a networked, outward-looking innovation culture*

Why?

Ideas get reviewed, adopted, rejected and improved faster than ever before. This means that any question requiring outside input gets feedback faster. Using the community increases the rate of innovation, while the right community will offer opportunities not considered before. Leveraging the community enhances your competitiveness as the community has more resources/competences/creativity.

How?

- Establish partnerships with various talent communities (universities, online) and crowd-sourcing platforms (Freelancer) to connect them with your teams to invent, analyse and implement new solutions (e.g. GE > Gaggle, BASF > universities).

- Acquire external competences through acquisitions.
- Partner with external start-up(s) or accelerators.
- Invest in start-ups that are doing what you want to do.
- Bring start-up veterans and project team members into the organisation to shift the culture from the inside.

The choice depends on scale, urgency and availability of solutions.

3. *Monitor technology breakthroughs, major customer behaviour changes, and experiment to find solutions.*

How?

Partner with start-ups and/or accelerators. Create small teams to evaluate, experiment, and eventually pursue options based on new technologies or new customer segments of existing applications. E.g. INTUIT (Quick books for self-employed in 2014). Effective experimentation depends on asking the right questions and streamlining the experiments through a professional experimentation group. A good way to experiment is to follow the process that Google follows:

- **Understand** the problem, the business, the context and the customer.
- **Diverge**. Generate insights and various potential solutions.
- **Converge**. Focus only on feasible ideas.
- **Prototype**. Build a prototype to be tested with existing or potential customers. A prototype is not

the final product, but a low-cost representation of the solution to be tested (e.g. Paper, PPT, Website, Video, 3D printing prototype)
- **Test and Learn**. Test the prototype with existing or potential new customers to get valuable feedback.

4. *Search actively for new business models*

A Business Model (BM) describes the elements and links of how an organisation or start-up *Creates, Delivers and Captures* Value. A Business Model consists of:

- Customer Value Proposition
- Customers, Channels and Customer Relationships
- Profit Formula (Revenue Streams and Cost Structure)
- Resources, Processes/Activities and Partnerships

In the past 50 years, the average business model lifespan has fallen from about 20 years to less than 10, if not even 5. Business model innovation is thus no longer one of many ways to gain a competitive edge, but it is a necessary core capability to respond to and capitalise on a changing world.

Why did business modelling become fashionable?

- Product Innovation could not realise the required growth targets.
- Apple, e-Bay and Amazon successfully demonstrated innovations in the business model.
- Business model innovations have cost-saving potential, potential to drastically change the rules of the game, new value creation, and finally, the

combination of new value creation with cost reduction, which is the essence of very successful business models.
- Internet penetration provided an enabler for many BM innovations.
- Xponentially growing technologies support innovative business models by enabling expansion of business to new industries while capturing value in the core business.

What are examples of major types of business models?

- *Multi-sided platform* with more than 1 type of user: Google, Uber, AirBnB
- *Long Tail*: Huge number of users selling small quantities (eBay, Netflix)
- *Free*: Advertising income pays for the product (Facebook, newspapers)
- *Freemium*: Basic service is free and pay for advanced (SKYPE, Spotify)
- *Consumables*: Printer/toner, razor/blades
- *Subscription services*: SaaS: Salesforce, Netflix
- *Transaction fees*: Square for payments, Airbnb for accommodation
- *Lead generation*: Groupon, you pay a commission fee for the leads
- *Marketplace*: Alibaba, connecting merchants to clients
- *eCommerce*: Amazon
- *Membership fee*: Great for cash flow
- *Membership fee and pay per usage*: Bike sharing companies, e.g. Mobike and Ofo, not yet proven successful.

1.4.1 Practical innovation methods

There are many ways to innovate and below is a description of four practical ways to innovate, namely generate new ideas and concepts. In Chapter 3, there will be in-depth description. The four methods are:

1. *Benefits of constraints/clear targets*

When you give a big constraint with clear targets to a TEAM, the creativity skyrockets. The result is innovative solutions with less resources within less time. We need clear targets, because *"whatever is measured is getting done."* This is what is happening with incentive competitions (e.g. crowdsourcing competitions). Additionally, if the team is set up in an isolated location (away from the mainstream business), the chance of coming up with more innovative concepts is higher.

2. *Mindset*

If you work on the mindset of your employees with the values/beliefs of the company, the results can be spectacular:

- "If it was easy, it would have been done," versus, "Everything is easy with the right tools and processes."
- "If anything can go wrong, it will go wrong," versus, "If anything can go wrong, fix it!"
- "We cannot predict the future," versus, "We cannot predict the future, so we will create it!"
- "We cannot improve," versus, "Measure it to improve it."

- "If you think something is impossible, then it is," versus, "Everything is possible."
- "No means no," versus, "No means maybe and find a different way to get yes."
- "Failure is failure," versus, "Failure is learning."

3. *Team roles exchange – different perspectives*

We start with the management team or with a multifunctional team and ask them to stand in a circle or sit around a round table.

- Ask all team members to start in their current role, each one in sequence explaining their challenges and for what they need help from others. The other persons write down the requests they receive for their own function.

- After all have finished the above for their own function, you ask all to assume another functional role. When each member has assumed a different functional role, you ask all members sequentially to explain their challenges and what they need from others in sequence in their new function. It is important for everyone to write down all ideas related to their function.

- After all, or partly all, have assumed all other functions, then they all go back to their original roles and each member commits two to three actions per function to improve their performance. Write all suggestions on a flip chart to find out how many great ideas you have generated.

The idea is that the different perspectives will generate a lot of good ideas and concepts.

4. *Create team collaborations and competitions*

Team characteristics: Small (5-6 people), youthful (mindset), younger people attempt the impossible; there is diverse knowledge/experience/culture/sex, risk taking, and failure is okay, and finally, clear targets with limited budget.

Multiple teams, 5-5-5-5 or 6-6-6-6; e.g. 5 teams with 5 people each, work for 5 weeks, to generate 5 ideas with limited budget. The rules are simple: failure is okay, best idea wins, if one team succeeds then all succeed (to enforce collaboration).

Another option is to use competition among the teams and after one or two elimination rounds to mix and match the best teams in later competition stages. This is an approach that INTUIT is using.

1.5 Summary

What do...Xponentially accelerating computer power, mobile Internet connectivity and artificial intelligence... urbanisation, aging population...new business models that demonetise, dematerialise and democratize... connected crowds that finance, create, solve and soon, everything else...all have in common?

They are the preconditions for a perfect storm.

Will technology impact jobs differently than in the past? This is difficult to be answered and there are so many books written about the subject. My answer is maybe, because based on history, new jobs will be created around the new technology (e.g. jobs between humans and machines, train machines, design with the help of machines, design AR/VR systems, design robots, ensure the proper use of AI, convert data to be suitable for input to an AI system).

Will your company survive the disruptive innovation that the storm will bring or will it survive against companies that create totally new markets which customers embrace fast? Figure 11 shows the average number of years a company stayed with the S&P 500 index. Although the average in 1960 was 60 years, in 2018, it is less than 20 years.

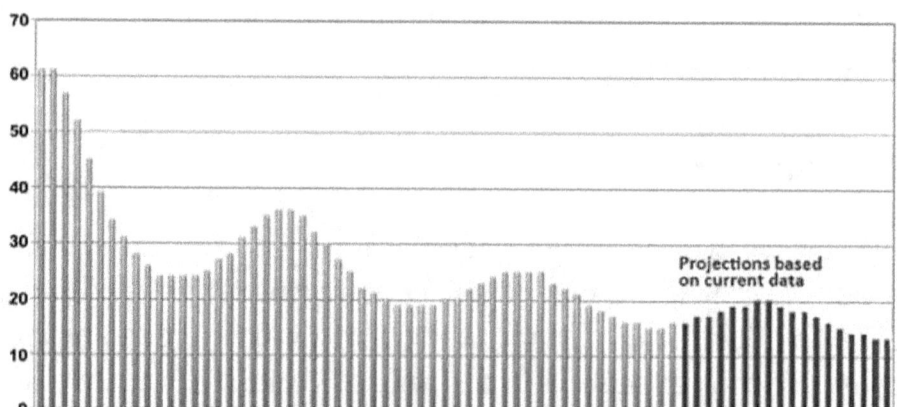

Figure 11

Companies like Nortel, Lucent and recently Nokia, Blackberry, Motorola and Yahoo are clear examples of the above effect.

Are you ready to embrace new opportunities? Do you know what to do? We have described the trends and the impacts of Xponentially growing technologies. Do you recognise them in your business? To evaluate if you and your company are ready for the era of Xponential growth, see a few relevant questions below:

- Are you, or is your company, thinking linearly?
- Which products or services are going to dematerialise or demonetise first in your industry?
- Which Xponential technologies are going to disrupt your business?
- What will become free in your industry in the future?
- What Xponential technologies can you use to create a competitive advantage?
- What Xponential technologies can you use to create new markets or business models, or expand industry boundaries?

Are you prepared for the era of Xponential growth?

Conclusion

- ***Information-based businesses (the number is increasing) are either growing Xponentially or becoming Xponentially more efficient.***
- ***The essence of any technological innovation is about the value that it brings to customers.***

Chapter 2: Understand the current business

As figure 12 shows, the 2nd step in your Xponential growth journey is to understand the current state of the business and the key characteristics of its business model. Beyond the strategic map creation method of understanding the current business described below, it is advised that the business model is also analysed using well-known tools like the business model canvas, which will not be explained here, as there is extensive literature on the subject. The business model canvas helps to evaluate the links among various business model attributes and more detailed financial analysis.

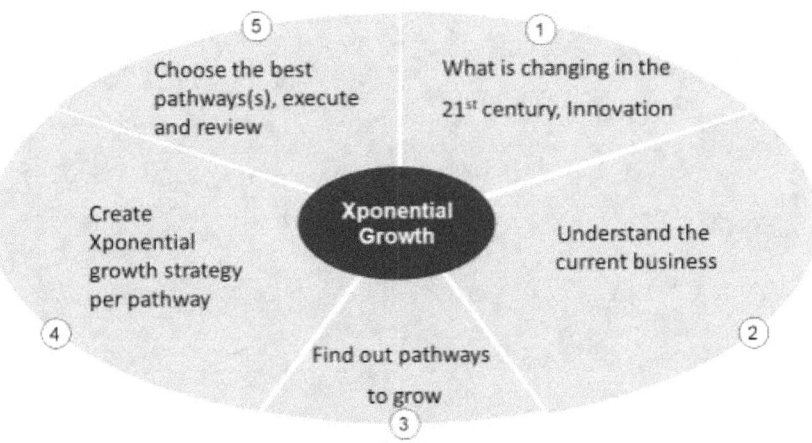

Figure 12

Every industry has its own factors of competition where every competitor is choosing where to focus to compete successfully. *Factors of competition are benefits or key features that are essential for the successful delivery of a product or service or experience to its intended customers.*

Typical Key factors of competition of many industries are: Quality, Location, Size, Technological advancement, Speed of delivery, Price, Unique industry-specific factors, Innovation in services, Ease of use, Ease of payment, Design.

As in the great majority of industries, the demand exceeds supply, and after some time the competitors become undifferentiated and finally end up competing with the same or similar factors of competition. Figure 13 shows what is normally happening. In such a situation, the profitability is declining and within a few years, many competitors start to lose money.

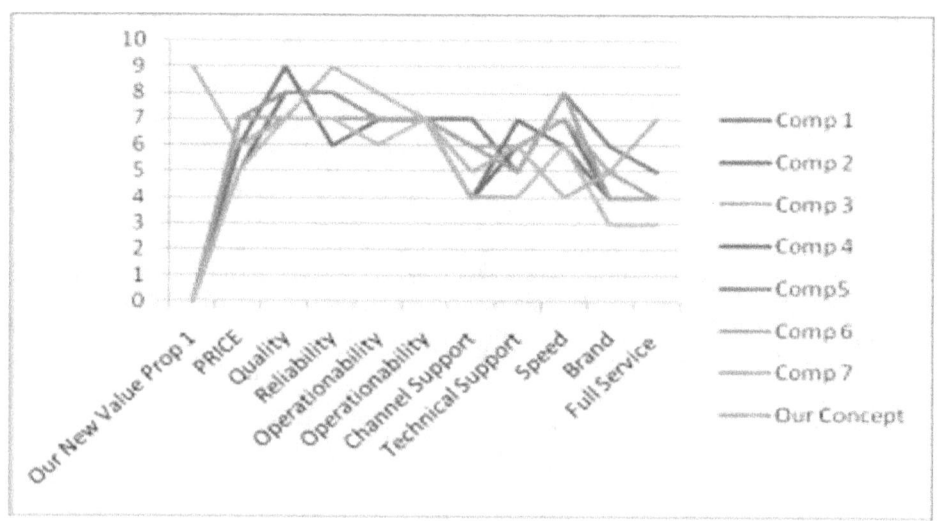

Figure 13

If a company introduces new factors of competition, it can create a totally new market where competition can become even irrelevant. The above can be compared to the fast food restaurant industry, where all compete with the same factors of competitions, versus the Michelin restaurants, where each is using different factors of competition and creating major differentiation. In this part of the Xponential growth journey, we will explain how to create the strategic map of the industry and then compare with the strategic map of your company or the company in concern. Such an effort needs a diverse and multifunctional team with broad industry experience. It is good practice to allow people to first work individually and then in a team in order to finalise this process step-by-step with better quality. Individual input ensures diversity of views, whereas in a team setting introverts are frequently discouraged from expressing their views or are suppressed.

There are three steps to be followed:

2.1 Identify and plot the key factors of competition of the industry.

A strategic map is a graph describing an industry's or a specific company's factors of competition in the horizontal axis with the levels (0-10 or 0-20, low to high) of these factors **as perceived from customers** *in the vertical axis.* This is to identify the factors of competition work, first individually, and then to share insights with the other team members. Write first the factors of competition on the horizontal axis. See figure 14 for the strategic map of the taxi industry.

Decide the level of the factors of competition (e.g. from 0- 10, low to high) in the team as *perceived from the customers* and plot the appropriate level from low to high on the vertical axis. It is essential to evaluate the level of competition as it is perceived from the customer and not your company's point of view. Plot similar levels of factors of competition close to each other to avoid the graph being an up and down waveform graph difficult to understand.

Do it first for the target industry as a whole, or the top two competitors. See below the first example about the taxi industry before UBER started their own business model. The key factors of competition selected are *cash payment, phone service, pricing stability, insurance policy, innovation in services and service orientation*. See details in Figure 14.

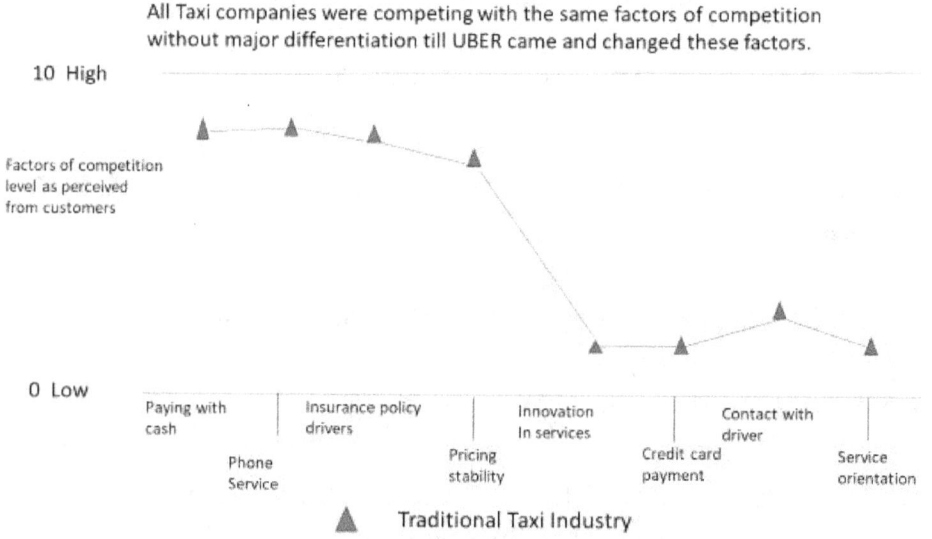

Figure 14, Strategic Map Taxi Industry

2.2 Draw your own company strategic map

The next step is to draw the strategic map of your own company. When UBER decided to enter the taxi business with a new business model enabled from new Xponentially growing technologies like mobile tech and apps as well as crowdsourcing (passengers and drivers), they changed the rules of the game. See Figure 15 on the following page, with the strategic map of UBER where the following changes or new factors of competition have been introduced:

- Cash payment >> only payments with a mobile app linked to credit card
- Phone service >> only taxi booking with an app
- From taxi driver employees >> taxi drivers self-employed
- High price stability >> to highly volatile price depending on demand
- Low innovation in services >> to increase in innovation in services
- No service orientation >> to very good service
- No driver contact >> to driver contact through the app

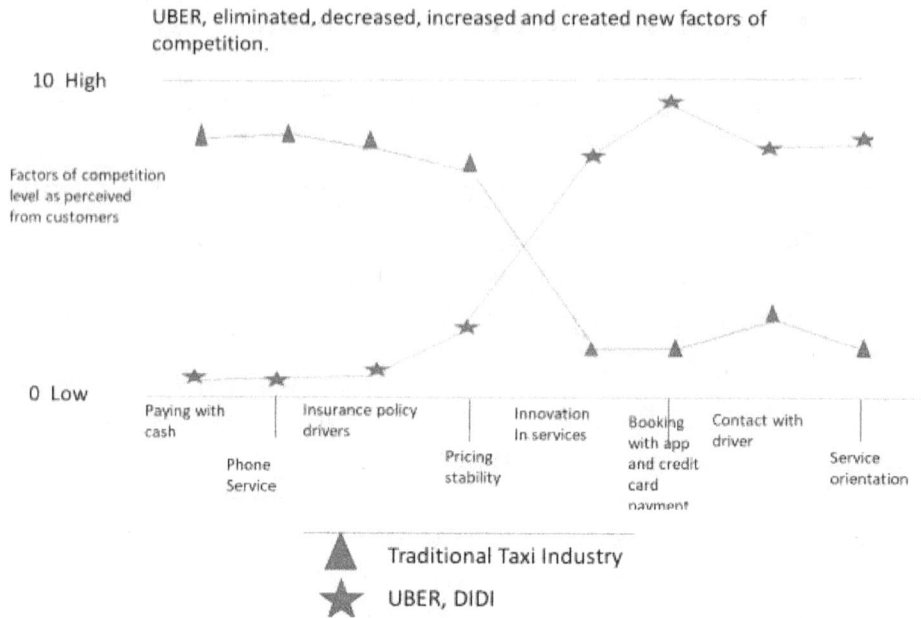

Figure 15, Strategic Map UBER and Taxi Industry

The results of the differentiating business model of UBER, with newly created factors of competition, have been appreciated by the customers and have resulted in tremendous growth of sales and skyrocketing valuation, reaching amazing levels—approximately $70 billion USD in 2018 within nine years from founding. In this case we should not forget that as the worldwide market is huge, the VC industry invested billions of USD.

2.3 Compare the strategic maps, discuss with team and draw your conclusions

In most of the cases in any mature industry, there is not much differentiation in the factors of competition between any company and the industry average, resulting in low or negative profitability, as almost all companies are competing with the same factors of competition. When any team assigned to create the strategic map is confronted with the hard reality of low differentiation, this is the moment that the change process begins. What is vital for the overall project is that the team that is entrusted to analyse the current business should be the same team that will later create and implement the future strategic map for reasons of believability, efficiency and accountability. In the case of two different teams, there is always a need to explain, and this can take time to reach consensus. There is the not "invented here" syndrome to be overcome and normally the team that needs to execute will be less motivated than the team that developed the strategy.

The availability of new technologies (mobile tech, crowdsourcing) has enabled UBER and later DIDI and other crowdsourcing transportation companies to create new factors of competition (mobile payments, mobile booking, knowing the vehicle position, and later on, use of data analytics to create new services (e.g. shared car services by knowing the location of various potential customers) as well as introduce better service orientation, *eliminate* cash payments, *increase* innovation in services and *decrease price* stability from high to low. Although in this case the new factors of competition are enabled from the new technologies. It is not always *technological changes* that enable innovation, but it can also be other attributes like:

- *Customer behavioural changes*
- *Regulatory changes*
- *Change the mix: functional versus emotional orientation of the industry*

- *Creation and introduction of new business models*
- *Eliminate customer blocking points and expand to new customer segments*

In order to understand better the process, see two more examples of strategic maps for two different industries below:

Mobile phone industry: At the time when Apple introduced the first two generations of iPhones, Apple created new factors of competition (touch screen, apps and Internet browsing), eliminated the hard keyboard and kept all the rest similar. Figure 16 shows the strategic map of iPhone versus the mobile phone industry as it was the case in 2008-2009.

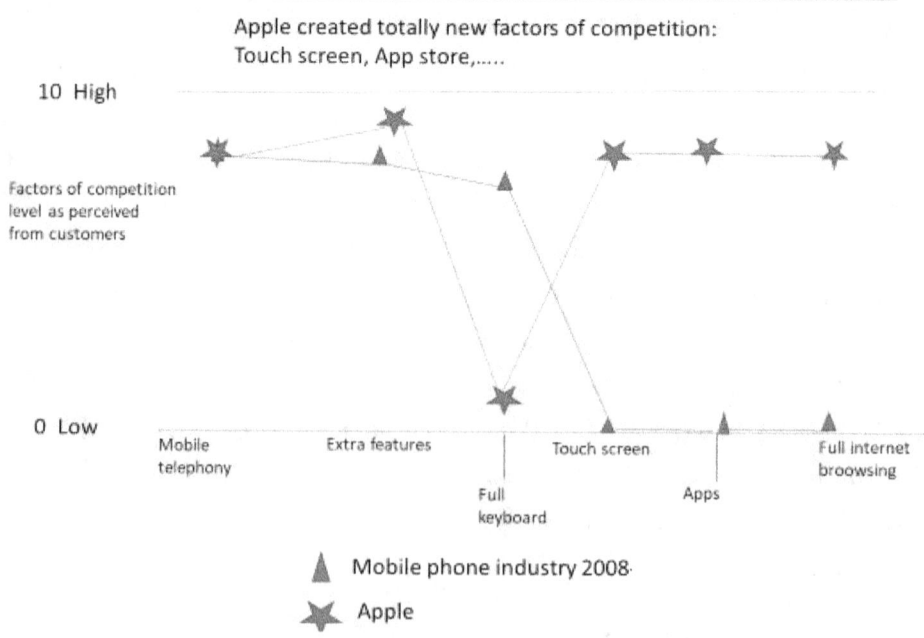

Figure 16, Strategic Map iPhone and Mobile industry

Social media industry: With Facebook, the incumbent, and Snapchat creating a new factor of competition (limited availability of past content) and increasing the speed and ease to upload content. See figure 17 for the strategic map of social media (Facebook and Snapchat)

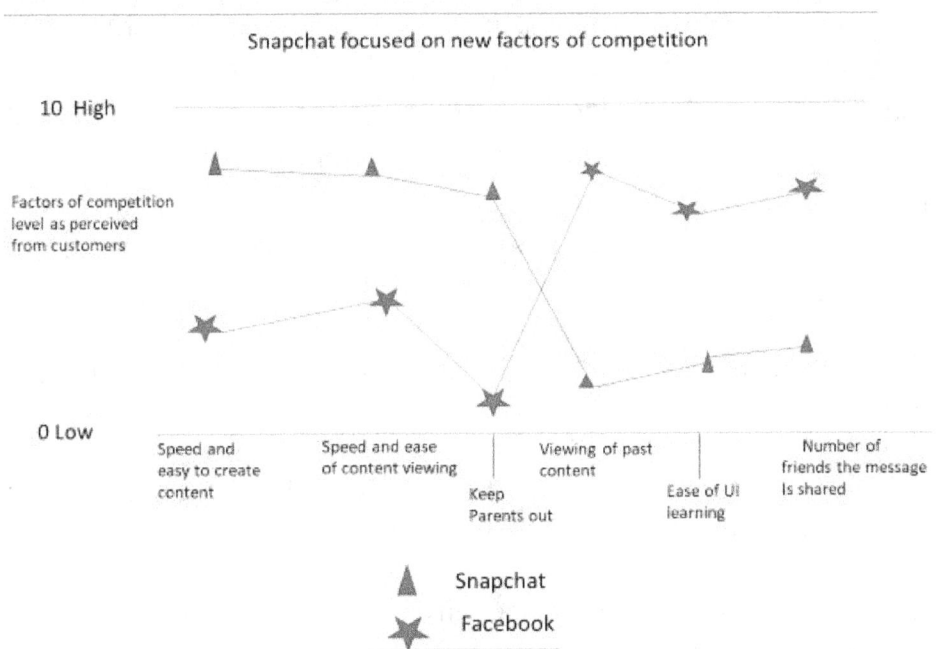

Figure 17, Strategic Map Social Media (Facebook, Snapchat)

Afterwards, the creation of a limited availability of past content is not as strong a factor of competition as it seemed initially, and consequently, the valuation of Snapchat has not grown as expected. This example shows how essential is to create totally new factors of competition instead of only increasing or decreasing the existing ones.

2.4 Summary and deliverables

In this part we have introduced the concept of the strategic map and the factors of competition. As we can appreciate from the three above-mentioned examples, the biggest impact is made from the creation of new, as well as elimination of existing factors of competition, and to a lesser extent, from the increase or decrease of the existing ones. We also need both creation of new factors of competition and elimination of existing ones to have new value AND lower cost at the same time. Only new value without elimination will not work, as the new business model will be most probably too expensive.

By the end of this process, there are two major deliverables:

1. The *strategic map* of the industry together with the strategic map of your own company.

2. A draft list of differences in factors of competition in four categories:

- Newly created factors of competition
- Eliminated factors of competition
- Increased factors of competition
- Decreased factors of competition

Conclusion

It is the combination of creation of new factors of competition AND elimination of other ones that will achieve great results.

Chapter 3: Find out pathways to grow

Before we talk about the process to find out pathways to grow, we will discuss the two major approaches for creating faster growth in any business. The first approach is to disrupt an existing market or industry by introducing a new value proposition or a new value-cost combination enabled from a new technology, or in general, a new business model. But what is the essence of disruption or *disruptive innovation*?

In the 20th Century, established companies have been caught-out by innovators (smaller companies with different technology or different value propositions and rarely with a different business model) entering and operating successfully at the lower end of their market or non-served market. These innovators, starting from low-end applications, have managed to work their way up as the incumbents reacted by vacating margin unattractive market segments and going upmarket. Technology and consumer expectation don't always go hand in hand (in almost any industry, the quality improves so much more than the customers' need, and consequently, the products or services become too expensive), leaving space for technology niches (often not yet mature enough) and therefore, mostly at the lower (margin unattractive) end of the market. E.g. Steel Industry: Mini Mills technology replaced initially the huge steel factories for simpler applications, and plastic household ware replaced metal ware for a number of applications. Focussed on the lower-end (higher volume) of the market, niche technologies manage to grow to mainstream adoption if they have intrinsic advantage(s) over the incumbent technology:

- Lower cost/less sophisticated, but better value
- Easier to develop and improve

If the niche technology focussed its market entry toward the non-consuming market, growth can go unnoticed by the incumbent for many years. e.g. the smartphone market has disrupted many portable PC manufacturers who thought that smartphones were not competing with PCs. Disruptive innovations often focus on finding alternative ways to get the job done and do not just suddenly happen. They take time to mature. If incumbents do not spot them, it is because they are not looking. They can also be anticipated. Not identifying the (tech) driver behind the disruptive innovation in time is fatal: Catching up may prove to be impossible. Going head-on with the innovator to avoid volume/scale loss, is in many cases the preferred strategy. Financial metrics are not geared to support such a strategy (you are going after low margin business). Disruptive innovations, especially the last 15 years, are not limited to technological innovations, but they focus more on the business models as we will find out. e.g. 3D printing will eventually affect retail, repair shops, logistics and many more parts of the existing value chains and emerging value networks, as we will see later on.

In summary there are three ways disruptive innovation took place in the 20th Century and until recently:

- Focussing on a lower cost, less sophisticated value propositions with unattractive gross margin for the incumbents
- Focusing on non-consumption
- Finding alternative ways to get the job done.

Although in the 21st Century, disruption is remaining a popular term and part of the normal technological progress, the focus is more on business model disruptions where real-time data and insights are becoming more and more essential. Normally, the result of any disruption is a zero sum game, where many people lose their jobs in the process, although other types of jobs are created. E.g. the manufacturing automation disruption with robotics, machine learning and AI is reducing, or will reduce the number of traditional manufacturing workers and at the same time, is increasing the number of engineering jobs related to design or maintenance of robots. In Chapter 1, we described many new technologies and their applications that are creating or will create disruptions. A lot of the time/disruptions are created because the incumbents are not innovating enough, leaving the space to new innovators to create innovative value-cost spaces resulting in disruption of their businesses. Companies like Amazon keep on experimenting (e.g. Amazon Go for convenience stores or Amazon Fresh for food delivery) and although many times these are failing (e.g. search engine or smartphones), many times they are succeeding (Kindle, AWS, Amazon Echo ecosystem of 4000 different devices).

But disruption is not the only way to do business in the 21st Century. There is the option to create new markets or even industries by solving big world problems, creating new demand, introducing new products, expanding the industry boundaries, and finally, expanding the potential customer population where existing players do not lose but the overall market expands. Water and energy shortages, environmental challenges, various diseases that kill millions and major healthcare cost increases when the percentage of older people is increasing are examples of big world problems. The next image, Figure 18, shows the 17 UN sustainable development goals related to many big world problems that need solutions and are inspirational for many new entrepreneurs.

Figure 18, 17 UN Sustainable Development Goals

Microfinance for financing small entrepreneurs, Viagra to extend the sex life of millions of couples, iTunes for enjoying digital music everywhere, Netflix for watching movies anywhere and AirBnB for renting spare rooms are examples of new products/services that created new markets and/or expanded the market. AirBnB has expanded the hospitality industry by utilising unused assets (spare rooms) and creating opportunities as well as expanding the travel market for young travellers who could not afford the normal hotel prices.

The bottom line is that you need to think not only in competition terms—which is natural, as you are part of an industry ecosystem with many participants, competitors and collaborators—but also, how to create something new or expand existing boundaries and create new demand.

For start-ups, it is natural to focus and create something new, many times disrupting and other times creating a totally new market. For established companies, you first need to analyse which part of your business you need to innovate. For the current business portfolio, incremental innovation is the norm and there is always a need to create a new future business portfolio for business sustainability.

As Figure 19 shows, the 3rd step in your Xponential growth journey is about finding options or pathways to grow. There are many ways to find pathways to grow, and before we move to this process, we need to first work on the mindset of the team members as well as for the team as a whole. Making the shift from linear to Xponential thinking, as well as broadening the mindset for what is possible is not an easy process; we need to devote adequate time, and a few inspiring principles help:

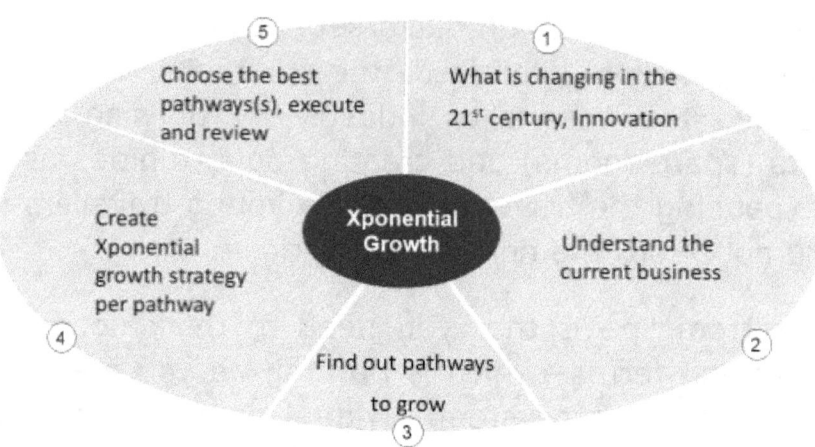

Figure 19

To succeed, we need to change and expand our thinking/mindset with what is possible, moving from something conventional >> TO something new. This is what I call **Growth Mindset.**

1. From competing in own market **TO expanding the market,**
2. From own industry **TO expand to other industries,**
3. From competing **TO make the competition irrelevant,**
4. From focusing only on existing demand **TO create new demand,**
5. From scarcity **TO abundance,**
6. From thinking in OR OR OR terms **TO AND AND AND terms** (e.g. new value creation AND cost reduction, faster AND cheaper AND better),

7. From limited product/service **TO solutions,** and
8. From product-centric **TO customer and experience - centric.**

At the same time, we need to prepare the team for the journey to become more resilient in order to succeed. Although the prospect of Xponential growth is very appealing, it needs the right approach, as people do not like change, especially big changes associated with Xponential mindset and growth. Internal politics and divisional silos are major hurdles, and finally, change needs the right motivation and determination to succeed. We need to find ways to reduce the above major hurdles. The following approach has worked in many reorganisations or growth businesses in which I have participated, and contains common success principles for major team efforts as well as can be found in various serious articles and books (e.g. *Blue Ocean Shift*, W. Chan Kim and Renee Mauborgne):

- *Involve all team members from the beginning, be open, acknowledge that the task is difficult and that with collaboration you will succeed.*
- *Ensure people discover and experience themselves the need for change as well as talking directly to customers and other ecosystem stakeholders.*
- *Assemble one team or teams that will do both strategy and execution to avoid the "not invented here" syndrome as well as be motivated to execute the strategy they developed.*
- *Split difficult tasks into smaller parts to create success and increase motivation.*

> *Create **Trust** among team members - see more about **Trust** and **Flow** on this website (www.businessdynamics.hk), guide people in the various process steps by explaining why we do what we do and what we can expect, as well as celebrate small successes during the journey.*

> *Treat all employees as equally important as all are important to deliver the company promise.*

> *In many successful organisations, a few management concepts are common success factors among many others:*

- Management is there to support employees to deliver their promise.
- Employees are company shareholders.
- Employees have bonuses linked to customer delight.
- Employee training is key to the organisation.

The mentioned mindset attributes are essential for success and it is advised to devote the necessary time to assemble the right team in the sense of skills and competences and create the conditions for people to embrace the right mindset, as well as create trust and flow among team members. After the above vital steps are satisfied, there are seven steps to be followed in this part of the process to find ways to grow the business by discovering and eliminating pain points or blocks, finding new ideas, expanding the group of potential customers and exploring various pathways.

3.1 Identify the pain points or blocks across the customer experience cycle

Below is a typical customer experience cycle with eight stages (see Figure 20). Depending on the industry, some stages might be substituted from other ones or some can be deleted.

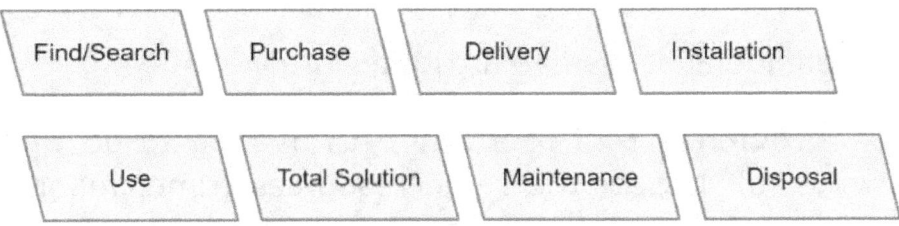

Figure 20, Customer Experience Cycle

Most businesses create products, services or experiences by focusing on two to three of these stages, copying industry practices for the rest or paying less attention. To potentially eliminate pain points or blocks and create new opportunities, we need to ask the right questions for these eight stages or those stages that are relevant from these eight, related to how the users experience utility in these stages. *Utility* is the state of being useful. To ask the right questions, we need to define suitable *utility attributes* that help to unlock blocks/pain points and create new opportunities to innovate and expand the market size. The most common utility attributes used in many similar concepts are:

- **Productivity**
- **Design**
- **Simplicity/Convenience**

- **Risk**
- **Society/Environmental Impact**
- **1 industry-specific attribute**

Five of these six are common utility attributes that apply for almost all experience cycle stages and the sixth one we leave open to be specific for the industry.

The definitions of the five attributes are:

- **Efficiency or Productivity:** Anything to do with use of less or the same resources (time, money, effort) to deliver the same or more value to the customer
- **Design:** Anything about style, looks, image, feel
- **Simplicity or Convenience:** Anything that simplifies things or gets things done faster and easier
- **Risk:** Anything related to risk reduction
- **Societal/Environmental Impact:** Everything about contribution or impact to society and/or environment

In order to discover pain points for each attribute and stage, you need to ask questions like, *What is the major block to the customer, or eventually, the opportunity for attribute X and why?*

Finally, we create a matrix with all the pain points/blocks and the relevant industry focus mentioned. This is called a customer utility matrix, with the horizontal axis showing the customer experience cycle stages and the vertical indicating the utility attributes.

For the taxi industry, before UBER, the focus was in using the taxi for point-to-point transportation, tolerating the low service orientation and not being able to pay with a credit card. By asking questions for the other experience cycle stages, we found pain points with:

- Delivery where there is low service image >> Design
- Purchase in not being able to pay with mobile >> Inconvenient
- Find/Search, need to call with waiting times and not knowing how far the taxi is >> Complexity

The same process can be applied for other industries.

3.2 Find out if these pain points or blocks limit any customers or potential customers

After the matrix has been completed, we ask the following questions to find out the impact of these pain points/blocks to existing customers or potential customers. Answers to these questions explain the importance of the various pain points:

- Does the industry impose pain points that could limit customer use of our product or service?
- Would existing customers move to a competitor who has eliminated these pain points?
- Would potential customers refuse to use and move to competition?
- Could these pain points discourage other potential customers from using our product or service?

The next step is to go with the team into the field to test and validate what you have learned from the matrix by interviewing customers or observing how real customers behave in the real world. The latter is essential, *as what people do is by far more important than what they say.* This process step is very important to understand the motivation behind customer preferences. Finally, you document customer feedback or observations. After you have identified the various pain points or blocks to potentially eliminate and what customers think about, the next step is to identify what potential new customer groups you could attract in order to expand your market.

3.3 Find out after elimination of pain points which new customer groups could attract

In every industry there are four major types of customers and potential customers:

- *Existing satisfied customers*
- *Dissatisfied existing customers*
- *Potential customers refusing to use your products/ services*
- *Potential customers that are unaware of your products/services or cannot afford your product/ service.*

To identify these customers and potential customers we ask three questions:

- Who of the existing customers use the products or services reluctantly?

- Who is refusing your products/services and uses the products/services of your competitors?
- Who could benefit from the industry but does not even consider it or it is too expensive for their budget?

In order to create a specification of the customer group profiles, you should follow the following process:

- Ask each member to compile their list individually and then share. It is great to make them visible on a flip chart showing the dissatisfied and potential customers.
- After discussion, each group should be aligned with the relevant category.
- Break into smaller teams and estimate the demand size of the various potential customer groups. Use Google and your own knowledge. The idea is to make rough estimations regarding the size of these groups.
- Share learning in the group by asking each member to express what they learned, which are the three groups (dissatisfied and potential customers) and their size relative to the existing customer group.
- Finally, when there is a consensus on the profile description and relative size of the three potential customer groups, the results are documented (see Figure 21).

Dissatisfied customers	Refusing potential customers	Unaware potential customers
Describe the profile or profiles of customers in this category as well as the market size e.g 12%	Describe the profile or profiles of potential customers in this category as well as the market size e.g 25%	Describe the profile or profiles of potential customers in this category as well as the market size e.g 35%

Figure 21, Customer Profiles

When there are various pain points and we need to decide to select some of them, we use criteria to evaluate which ones are the most important to focus on. To achieve that, we use the following two attributes:
Importance (give a score from 0-10); Satisfaction (give a score from 0-10)

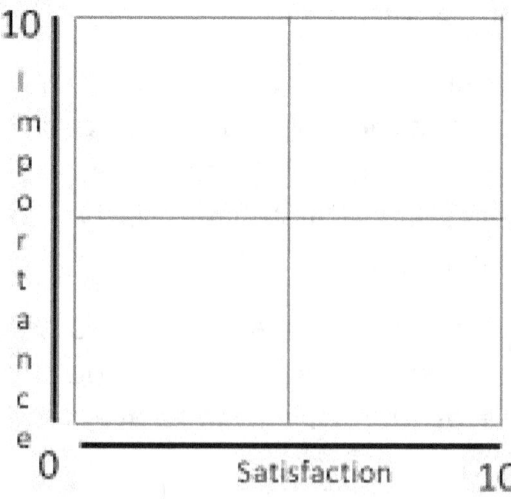

Figure 22, Importance/Satisfaction

Then plot all pain points/needs in a matrix (see Figure 22 (importance and satisfaction)) and evaluate based on the two rules mentioned below, applying them separately for the various potential customer groups:

- *When there is a pain point or need that has a high importance score and low satisfaction, it is a good opportunity for new value creation.*
- *When there is a pain point or need that has a low importance score and high satisfaction, it is a potential opportunity for cost reduction.*

After you have identified the most promising pain points to be eliminated, converge and conclude by answering the questions in step four.

3.4 Decide what pain points to eliminate and which customer and potential customer group(s) to focus

Having identified the most important pain points to convert to an opportunity and which customer or potential customers to focus on, it is the right time to find the best combination of these two key attributes by asking the following questions:

- Which of the previous three customer profiles has the highest potential to develop big market and growth?
- Are there any links between the discovered blocks to utility and any of the three customer profiles?
- What will be the impact of eliminating blocks to the three customer profiles?

- What is missing from the industry offerings that, if included, could unlock new demand?

With answers to these questions any company could improve their value propositions, create new value and increase demand by addressing new groups of potential customers. A company could decide to implement the changes and test the market or move forward and develop more value to accelerate Xponential growth. Figure 23 below explains the two options:

If Option 1 is chosen, then the chosen combination of improvements with a specific customer group is validated in the market with real customers (talk and observe) followed by potential further improvements and implementation of the changes to grow the business. If Option 2 is chosen, then the next step is to understand better and in more depth innovation in the Xponential 21st Century. In most of the cases, Option 1 will be implemented first, followed by Option 2.

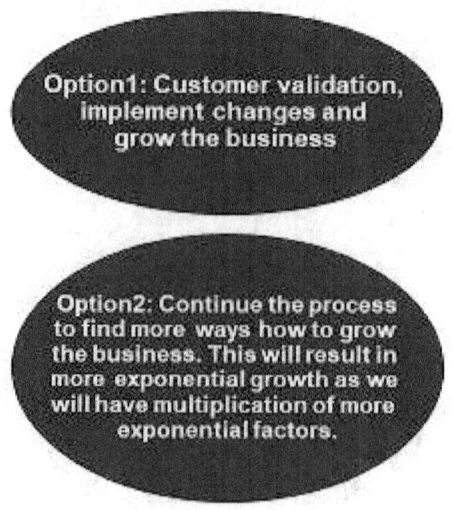

Figure 23

3.5 Understand better innovation in the Xponential 21st Century

After we have already seen what is changing in the 21st Century, Figure 24 summarises the major shifts taking place in the world.

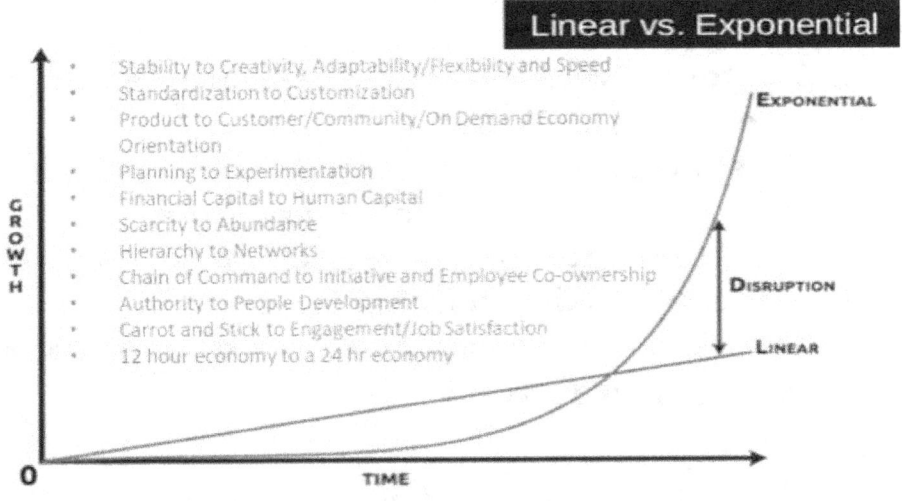

Figure 24

Major changes like the shifts described above, as well as what we have seen in Chapter 1, mean that innovation as we know it and apply so far needs to be enriched with new **Success Factors**. The new success factors are:

- *Understanding that the world has changed*
  - *Power of the individual and crowd*
  - *The need to learn new things more frequently*
- *Speed (vaguely right vs precisely wrong)*
- *Scale faster*
- *Agility, flexibility, adaptability*
- *Asset light, leverage of assets*
  - *Data*

o *3rd party assets*

Translating the above success factors by asking what will help established companies to innovate in an Xponential world as well as taking into account the learning from Chapter 1, is equivalent to how to become as lean, agile and focused as a start-up, and the *innovation principles* become:

1. **Create a transformative purpose, embrace autonomy and speed**
2. **Big scale performance targets**
3. **Embrace the crowd and communities**
4. **Re-design your innovation set-up**
5. **Leadership/learn new skills**
6. **Be prepared to change, pivot everything when you are wrong**

3.5.1 Define a transformative purpose, embrace autonomy and speed
Why?

A transformative purpose attracts talent, creates a community around and enables you to compete better. It is transformational in the sense that it inspires employees and other stakeholders to do great work. According to new university research both in the USA and the UK, the 21st Century motivators are *Purpose, Autonomy* and *Mastery* and there is need for a higher aspirational purpose that captures the hearts and minds of those both inside and outside of the organisation. The link https://youtu.be/rrkrvAUbU9Y is an excellent video explaining the above-mentioned 21st Century motivators. The greater connectivity and new technologies allow for unprecedented speed of access and decision-making, and that is why there is a need for more autonomy and less, or no, hierarchy.

3.5.2 Big scale performance targets

Xponential technologies are not about incremental improvement. They are about radical and huge improvements in something. Despite the fact we are generally resistant to change, we will always continue to adopt things that are better by 10X or even more. This means that solving problems that make our lives 10X better will be always in demand. Moreover, the Xponentially growing technologies allow us to make the shift to Better AND Bigger AND Faster AND Cheaper instead of the traditional Better OR Faster OR Cheaper. A few examples help us to understand this:

- Smartphones, including all functions, are better AND cheaper AND easier to use than previous phones and all devices they replaced, like IPod, camera, navigation system or video recorder.

- WhatsApp and Wechat are cheaper AND easier to use AND offer more variety of functions than traditional mobile phones.

- Drones for many applications are cheaper AND faster to deploy AND easier to use: Taking pictures for big agricultural areas or for checking progress of big real estate projects versus other methods like the use of helicopters or people.

- Automotive industry: In the future it is expected that autonomous vehicles used for taxis will be cheaper AND offer better service AND be safer than current taxis.
- Upcoming supermarkets or coffee shops will be automated with less people and no cashiers etc., will be cheaper AND easier to shop in AND be faster to check out than current supermarkets.

Before we explain the third principle, embracing crowd and communities together with the increasing shared economy trend are major changes to how we will innovate. We will start now with the principle *embrace the crowd and communities* (see Figure 25, defining Crowd versus Community).

Figure 25, Crowd versus Community

3.5.3 Embrace the crowd and communities
Why?

This is an important subject and here we will go into more depth: Ideas get reviewed, adopted, rejected and improved faster than ever before. Using the community increases the rate of innovation, while the right community will offer opportunities not previously considered. Leveraging the community before others enhances your competitiveness as the community/ crowd have more resources/ competences/ creativity. Embracing a social and environmental purpose is supporting community creation.

There are three steps to building a community from a crowd:

- *Use a transformative purpose to attract the right people,* e.g. TED, Tesla, GitHub
- *Nurture the community*: Devote time, listen, provide value, content, games, create an app, incentive competitions, e.g. drone communities, meetups.
- *Create a platform to automate a peer-to-peer community*, e.g. Reddit, Uber, Airbnb

Finally, there are a number of attributes related to crowd and communities for which I will elaborate below:

1. Staff on demand

Get experts that don't work for you, maximise flexibility (e.g. Freelancer, Mechanical Turk, Fiverr), and finally, reduce fixed costs. P&G is using the Gigwalk platform to place merchandise on the Walmart shelves.

2. Leverage 3rd party assets

Fast prototyping, using specific equipment that otherwise could not be afforded: Prototypes (Techshop or equivalent), many successful devices have been created with Techshop resources in the USA, e.g. the Square device (mobile payments). On-demand economy generally supports third party qualitative and competitive leverage of assets: Cloud computing (Amazon, Rackspace).

3. Customer involvement, experimentation/engagement

Many new (virtual or augmented reality) technologies support better experimentation during the creation process with customers, including constant iteration, increasing the chance of success. Engagement is improving through better user experience, sharing of content, using incentive prizes, and finally, using games to attract potential customers.

4. Autonomy

The greater connectivity and the new technologies allow for unprecedented speed of access and decision-making. For a company to remain competitive, it needs to be able to match the speed through more autonomy (people and automation), especially at the organisational edges.

5. Social Technologies

To remain competitive, improve collaboration and grow the community, you need to automate: File sharing (e.g. Dropbox), cloud document management and collaboration tools both for for internal use (Slack) and with the community.

6. Automation and Algorithms

Leveraging the massive number of data that is accessible through new technologies and the greater connectivity will result in better customer insights (through better algorithms), improvement of the user experience, and finally, more efficient company operations. UPS is using more than 60000 vehicles to make more than 18 million deliveries per day by using telematics and algorithms. In this way, the rerouting is more efficient, saving billions of USD per year.

7. Reward crowdfunding

It is about preselling a product or service. With this process, you are, in fact, getting paid in advance by promising to deliver a product or service to potential customers within a number of months. It is not only about financing your R&D and the start of the go-to market but it is even more important to the validation of the product/system/service concept in a very direct and cost-effective way. There are so many examples of successful projects; e.g. through Kickstarter, PEBBLE raised from tens of thousands of USD up to $20 million USD (2015 Pebble TIME watch) by preselling products. Not all crowdfunding campaigns raise millions; the most are in the range of tens of thousands of USD, and the feedback/validation of the concept is very valuable.

What are the key reward crowdfunding steps?

The reward Crowdfunding process is a marketing campaign with the following steps:

- To reach out to the crowd and create a community is the responsibility of the start-up. The crowdfunding platform does not create the community—the start-up does.

- Evaluating the right amount of money to be raised is crucial.

- Create a strong group of affiliates before the start of the campaign that will support the funding campaign actively in the beginning.

- Choose the various rewards ($10 USD (supporting the cause), to a basic product, step-up product or system, and a few different colour versions to be tested in the campaign).

- Test all rewards with people before the campaign starts.

- It is really a marketing campaign and needs to be executed from a team of competent professionals.

- For a successful campaign, a start-up needs to reach 30 % of the target amount on the first day and above 50% within the first two days. Moreover, 30-40 days is a good time for completion.

- Depending on the industry/product/service, you may execute a campaign in one go or through a few sub-campaigns, like first introducing a simple product and then a second, more elaborate one.

8. *Equity crowdfunding*

With equity crowdfunding, investors are buying equity from a company rather than buying the company's product or services. A product/system/service proven from the customers' demand though Kickstarter or Indiegogo or other equivalent platform will be much easier to be accepted through an equity crowdfunding platform or a VC, e.g. Crowdfunder or Wefunder. As the industry is new, there is a lot of innovation in the space and minimum regulatory requirements in various countries are catching up.

3.5.4 Re-design your Innovation set-up

For the innovation set-up, there are a few options. See the various descriptions below:

1. *Create new business*, a standalone unit, autonomous and reporting to the CEO. Do not integrate with the old business (internal politics will create many obstacles) until the new business is scaling fast and then evaluate how to leverage the rest of the company. For the initial team, use the most innovative employees (free and open thinkers) you have and add a few new ones (from outside) to create the right diversity and enhance competence. The new business portfolio/future businesses are set up separately, (incubator setup and/or start-ups are acquired to become part of the incubator) working to discover a viable business model before they run out of cash.

This approach is essential, as working within a big company, the start-up culture needs to be preserved.

Your focus is to innovate by creating new businesses based on new business models or develop new value innovations based on new technologies or a combination of both.

The current businesses are focusing to delight existing customers, defend existing margin structure, grow and generate income to support the organisational objectives at large. These businesses are normally big with an established customer base; go to market channels and processes. These are major assets for an established company and any disruptor would love to have these assets. Your focus is to innovate and grow the business within their market segments and product portfolio without creating new business beyond their core. As big businesses are not normally flexible enough to behave like start-ups or compete with start-ups, they focus mainly on Routine/Sustaining/Incremental Innovation. For start-ups, aligning the employee metrics with the organisational purpose and using the right metrics for innovation is key. Metrics for new businesses are different from those for established businesses:

- Start with growth metrics (e.g. leads generated, number of early adopter customers that bought the MVP, monthly burn rate).

- Add traditional value metrics (revenue and profit) only after scalability is proven and sales organisation is established.

2. *Partner with external innovator(s)/start-ups.* This is a good way to create external focus and learn.

3. *Invest in start-ups or accelerators* that are doing what you want to do. It is a good option to learn and decide later for a potential acquisition, e.g. **Google** invested first and acquired NEST later as the unit that started and expanded the focus for entering the home business. Google and Apple are investing or acquiring start-ups very frequently.

4. *Let start-ups find your weak spot.* **Cisco** finances with VCs (e.g. Sequoia Capital or PwC) start-ups to test and potentially disrupt their own group strategy or create a business in a market segment where Cisco cannot compete. If successful, they acquire them.

5. *Set up Innovation outposts*. Larger companies may decide to set up innovation centres in locations where innovation is happening (e.g. Silicon Valley, Israel, Shenzhen, Beijing) with the following focus:

- *Invent:* You establish project-specific advanced development efforts, like BMW or Verizon's Silicon Valley R&D centre focuses on big data and software technologies or investigate technologies and business models the innovation ecosystem is known for in order to create new products and services.

- *Invest:* You allocate a corporate venture fund that invests in start-ups working on technology and/or business model innovations of interest.

- *Incubate:* You support the efforts of very early stage teams and companies that want to develop solutions in areas of interest; for example,

Samsung's incubator focuses on start-ups working on the Internet of Things.

- *Acquire:* Companies buy start-ups in order to access both the innovations the start-ups are developing and their employees, and in the process, inhibit competitors from getting them. For example, Google acquired several of the robotics start-ups that had what was considered to be the best intellectual property.

- *Partner:* Collaborate with start-ups in order to develop a disruptive new solution using their innovations along with the corporations, or to distribute innovative solutions the start-up has developed. For example, a few years ago, Mercedes partnered with Tesla in batteries for electric vehicles.

There are three stages to set-up innovation outposts that work, and in each stage people with different qualifications are needed:

- *1st phase*: Networking and Partnering: The initial tasks of the new innovation outpost are to monitor technologies, innovations and business models for specific innovation areas. At this stage, you need competent business development people looking for innovations that could become threats that could lead to the disruption of the business or could allow the corporation to be disruptive by entering adjacent markets to the ones it currently serves, or finally, could create and introduce new or disruptive offerings for new markets.

- *2nd phase: Invest, Invent, incubate, acquire or partner*: In this phase, you need more VC and M&A types of people, and the various options have been covered before.

- *3rd phase: Productise a solution in the innovation outpost:* What is important is to have clear agreement about the productisation with the headquarters of the corporation.

3.5.5 Leadership/learn new skills

The leadership of the organisation needs to be educated about the new Xponentially growing technologies and any changes due to the growth of the shared, collaborative and on-demand economy. It is, in fact, lifelong learning and the Coursera top courses in 2017 (33 million learners worldwide in 2017) were: machine learning, neural networks and deeper learning, learning how to learn, introduction to mathematical thinking, bitcoin and cryptocurrency technologies, programming for everybody, algorithms part 1, and English for career development.

Concerning the difference in mindset between the younger generation and the current leadership one, attention is needed: *They want to learn, they want to be spontaneous, they want to feel "free" and they want to have an "up-side" in the value they are creating.* Successful leadership needs:

- Implementation of more leadership diversity (age, male/female, competence and cultural)

- Promotion of faster, younger people in leadership or co-leadership positions to leverage the new mindset and knowledge.

3.5.6 Be prepared to change, pivot everything when you are wrong

The greatest gift that the Internet, and in general, the connected economy gives to any individual or business is the opportunity to fail faster at a lower cost. Continuous and fast experimentation to find a winning business model is essential for success.

To analyse your current innovation capabilities and systems, please refer to the questionnaire in Exhibit 2 at the end of this book. After the evaluation of where you stand as a company, it is essential to think about how to find out new ideas and concepts leveraging the Xponential culture.

3.6 Innovation in the future/Xponential culture/how to generate new concepts

Creativity and innovation is vital in any era and the question about how to generate new ideas and concepts in the 21st Century becomes very relevant. As the two key attributes of the era in which we live are **Disruptive** and **Xponential,** we need to explore their characteristics.

Let's start with **Disruptive**. In the 20th Century the disruptions were slow, could be prevented with the right strategy, and the main focus was on lower cost/margin solutions as well as addressing no consumption. In the

21st Century, the digital disruptions are very different. They are **faster** (Google navigation software disrupted the HW-based navigation industry, Tom Tom and Garmin within months), they have a much **bigger** impact in the sense that they even have the power to dematerialise and demonetise industries (Whatsapp, Uber, Airbnb), are based on **lower cost experimentation** and flexible crowd resources (Cloud), and finally, are many times focused on **business models** change.

Summarising the characteristics of *Disruptive Innovations* in the 21st Century:

- **They are often based on low-cost experimentation using existing technologies/platforms, many times unplanned and from a few people.**
- **They reinterpret and modify existing business models.**
- **Adoption is faster as customers communicate much faster. No need really to always cross the chasm.**
- **Most of the time they have better performance AND lower cost AND better customer experience.**
- **They leverage crowd resources and virtually integrated supply chain (cloud).**

We have also observed that there are a few key characteristics of the 21st Century that are Xponential in nature, and we call them **Xponential Business Culture.** We have extensively covered the Xponential nature of many technologies and resulting applications, and these characteristics are:

- **Big Scale/Big Purpose**
- **Autonomy and Speed**
- **Community and Crowd**
- **Xponentially Growing Technologies**
- **Data Based Insights**

Combining the characteristics of **Disruptive Innovations** in the 21st Century with **Xponential Business Culture** characteristics, we create a matrix, which we call **Xponential Culture Matrix,** with questions that can inspire any company to generate new ideas and concepts. The questions are general and adaptable to the specific market or industry context. Some of the questions seem too general or abstract until the specific context is taken into account.

The 25 generic questions to generate new ideas and concepts are to be found in Exhibit 1. Many of the ideas generated from the questions of the Xponential Culture Matrix can be used in the strategy development for growth, as well as specifically to enrich the eight growth pathways we will explore next.

3.7 Identify new value creations and cost reductions by analysing the eight pathways

After analysing the mindset needed for innovation in the 21st Century and creating the Xponential Culture Matrix to find new ideas and concepts, what follows are the growth pathways. I have selected eight pathways that lead to various options for growth. As some of these ideas have exponential nature while others are linear, when we combine ideas or concepts and multiply them, we can create faster Xponential growth.

The eight pathways to be explored are:

1. **Evaluate other industries solving the same problem.**
2. **Evaluate other companies with different positioning in the same industry.**
3. **Evaluate the types of customers across the value chain.**
4. **Evaluate the total solution.**
5. **Explore the functional/emotional orientation of your industry.**
6. **Evaluate new technologies and their applications.**
7. **Apply AND, AND, AND instead of OR, OR, OR and find out what can change substantially in your value/cost balance.**
8. **Reinterpret, modify existing business models and create new digital ones.**

In the rest of this chapter, we will explore the "how-to" of these eight pathways to find options to grow. The idea is to use an expanded mindset and avoid the standard methods of competing better against competitors within the same industry. Not all eight pathways will give viable options for growth for a specific business, but the systematic process of approaching growth from so many different pathways as well as combining with ideas from the Xponential Culture Matrix will create Xponential growth through the

Xponential nature of some of the pathways and Xponential technologies, as well as the multiplication effect of the Xponential growth pathways.

3.7.1 Evaluate other industries solving the same problem

You first identify the major problems or needs your industry solves and find which alternative industries solve the same problems or address similar needs. Then you ask people why they choose one alternative over the other (e.g. train over bus or plane, or DIY channel versus hiring a professional to repair something at home) and which industry catches the majority of customers. This is a focus area for comparing main alternative industries versus your own industry. Then you find the positive and negatives of the different alternatives by asking customers from your industry AND other industries the following questions:

- What are the main factors of your own industry versus the main alternative industries that made the customer choose your own industry?
- What are the main factors of your own industry versus the main alternative industries that made the customer choose against it?

Document the insights gained from asking the aforementioned questions, especially the reasons why people made choices, and start to document which factors of competition need to be:

- Eliminated
- Decreased

- Increased
- Created

3.7.2 Evaluate other companies with different positioning in the same industry

Evaluate other major companies within your industry with different positioning or business models and focus on the top two dominant types relevant to your own positioning (e.g. the hotel industry has various levels of hotels at 5* or 4* or 3*; the restaurant industry has various levels of quality/service levels; or examples also exist in any other industry that offers various levels of services or product sophistication offering similar value proposition). The idea is to find the key factors that made a customer choose a different level of service or product sophistication, especially nowadays, where in almost any industry there are new value propositions and business models appearing—from the media industry, to consumer electronics, to the car industry. To find this out, you interview the customers of these companies with different positioning or business models and find out why they choose certain companies and reject others. Ask questions like:

- Why do you choose this value proposition?
- Why do you reject the alternative?
- Do you make any compromises? How could the company support you to eliminate them?
- Any other observations?

Document the insights from the mentioned questions, especially the reasons why people decide on a certain choice and start to document which factors of competition need to be:

- Eliminated
- Decreased
- Increased
- Create

3.7.3 Evaluate the types of customers across the value chain

Identify the chain of customers (e.g. users, purchasers, influencers, decision makers), and shift away from the main customer group to other neglected groups (e.g. Purchasing VP versus CIO or CFO). Normally, Purchasing, CIO and CFO have a different definition of value for the same value proposition. The Purchasing VP will focus on the purchase price or monthly subscription fee, the CIO on the benefits it brings to the IT department, and finally, the CFO might focus on the maintenance cost of a software package (not SaaS) or on disposal costs for a hardware product. To find out, interview untargeted customers and find out insights and different definitions of value.

Ask questions like:

- What are the biggest pain points/ costs/ inconveniences/blocks to utility that the industry's current value proposition imposes on you?
- How could we eliminate or reduce them for you?
- What would the ideal value proposition look like if we focused on you versus the customer group on which the industry currently focuses?

Document the insights from the mentioned questions and start to document which factors of competition need to be:

- Eliminated
- Decreased
- Increased
- Created

3.7.4 Evaluate the total solution

Observe customers using the product or service before, during and after purchase. Use the customer utility map to check out relevant blocking points. Identify the typical growth strategy for products that use other supplements in order to function (coffee machine uses coffee and water or cooking devices use oil or other ingredients). Observe customers using the products and ask questions before, during and after use of the product or service like:

- What are the biggest pain points/costs/inconveniences/blocks to utility in each stage?
- What do you observe as blocks in the three stages, before, during and after use?
- Are there any major blocks that when eliminated can access potential customer groups that are not accessible now?

Document the insights from the mentioned questions and start to document which factors of competition need to be:

- Eliminated
- Decreased

- Increased
- Created

3.7.5 Explore the functional/emotional orientation of your industry

Starting with the industry's current orientation, define whether it is functional or emotional. Ask customers and potential customers for three to five adjectives or characteristics describing the industry. The idea is to change the industry's orientation to create a totally new value proposition and potentially a new business model. Explore what the opposite characteristics would be if the industry changed orientation, and what that would mean to value creation. What would be the best words to describe this new industry?

Imagine how any functional industry, like medical, legal or financial, could transform if emotional elements are added in the way they operate. The other way around, you can see how social face-to-face, connection-related industries can change to very functional, with full AI automation and interaction through smart devices.

Document the insights from the interaction with customers and start to document which factors of competition need to be:

- Eliminated
- Decreased
- Increased
- Created

3.7.6 Evaluate new technologies and their applications

Evaluate which new technologies are gaining a lot of traction in relevant applications, are irreversible, and which new technologies will impact your business model. Then ask the following questions:

- What technologies can you use to create a competitive advantage?
- Which products or services are going to dematerialise or demonetise in your industry because of the applications the new technologies enable?
- Which Xponential technologies are going to disrupt your business?
- What is going to become free in your industry?

Use the answers to the questions from the **Xponential Culture Matrix** to find out more ideas to create new value and reduce cost.

Document the insights from the questions and start to document which factors of competition need to be:

- Eliminated
- Decreased
- Increased
- Created

3.7.7 Apply AND, AND, AND instead of OR, OR, OR and find out what can change substantially in your value-cost balance

Evaluate where in the past you have been limited in your business model with OR choices and test if changes to AND, AND creates different or better value proposition, and then do the same for the other attributes of the business model. Finally, evaluate whether AND, AND can even enable change for the business model and ask customers to validate your assumptions.

Document the insights from the above analysis and start to document which factors of competition need to be:

- Eliminated
- Decreased
- Increased
- Created

3.7.8 Reinterpret, modify existing business models and create new digital ones.

Using the business model canvas, describe your existing business model or outline the dominant industry business model. Describe the core principle of the business model and create a list of all the key assumptions where the key business model elements are based. Steps 1, 2 and 3 below are three different ways to start the creation of a new business model or modify an existing one. Steps 4-9 are needed to complete it.

1. Create a powerful customer value proposition by focusing on a job to be done addressing barriers related to: *Wealth* (e.g. lower cost cars like the Tata Nano), *Access* (e.g. Hilti tools), *Skill* (e.g. QuickBooks) and *Time* (e.g. minute clinics). To create the value proposition, start from customer needs (functional) and wants (emotional) first and then translate these needs and wants to benefits/features of the job to be done.

To create a powerful value proposition, pay attention to the following:

- Strengthen the *Relative advantage* of the product or service over the status quo;
- Build in *Compatibility* with what customers already do;
- Reduce *Complexity* of communicating benefits (is it easy to understand?);
- High *Observability* of benefits (can customers observe others?);
- *Low risk of failure* (functional, social, financial risk); and
- Enable *trials* (small number of units).

2. **Reframe an industry** by examining its foundation and make changes in line with changes in customer behaviours/needs and/or reversing conventional wisdom. Create a few business model (BM) disruptions by drastically changing the core principle with "what if" questions, or ask questions like:

- Which of the factors that the industry takes for granted should be eliminated?
- Which factors should be reduced below the industry standard?
- Which factors should be increased well above the industry standard?
- Which factors should be created that the industry has never offered?
- Is there a far better way?

Examples of core principle change or applying other industry business models are:

- From product invention and innovation being created within a company, to innovation being created through an online community of people (Fiverr, Upwork, Spigit);

- From economies of scale viability to long tail, where the network made it possible to sell low volumes per item for a huge number of users (eBay);

- From in-house assets to using third party assets (Computational resources: Amazon, Rackspace. Prototypes: Techshop);

- From consumer research to data analytics insights (Palantir);

- From customer validation limited face-to-face tests, to customer validation and financing through online communities (Kickstarter and Indiegogo); and

- From financing through venture capital to financing through crowdfunding (Wefunder, Crowdfunder).

3. Test applicability of business models from other industries.

- From a multi-sided business model in the online hospitality booking industry (Airbnb), to the transportation industry (Uber) (other industry business model); and

- Same as above for bike sharing (Mobike, Ofo) with the addition of an upfront payment.

4. Design a new profit formula.

5. Assemble the right resources to deliver the value proposition profitably.

6. Create processes and later, metrics, to make the delivery of the value proposition repeatable and scalable.

7. The combination of the right resources and processes creates a competitive advantage.

8. Use the business model canvas where you can combine and recombine capabilities.

9. Decide about a version of the new business model and test it in the real world. Learn, change and test again.

In the 20th Century, we analysed linear value chains to understand the value creation as well as value movements and exchanges within business ecosystems. The exchanges were simpler, with mainly products or services being delivered, and money was flowing in the opposite direction. In the 21st Century, and as the economy is becoming more connected, more global, more complex and more digitised, we are moving from value chains to *Value Networks* and *Digital Business Models*.

A value network or ecosystem is defined as a value-creating system in which all involved stakeholders (people, companies, institutions, governments) co-produce value. The platform technology enables this co-production. This fact gave rise to the *Platform Business*

Model, which is a way to create, deliver and capture value that is co-produced among the stakeholders in the network (e.g. Uber, Wechat, Facebook, AirBnB, Mobike). See the example of the value network of a technology provider in Figure 26 on the following page.

In the 21st Century, value network participants are co-creating value with complex network interactions, including many different flows:

- Products or services
- Financial flows
- Information flows
- Intangible flows related to reputation or opinions or brand

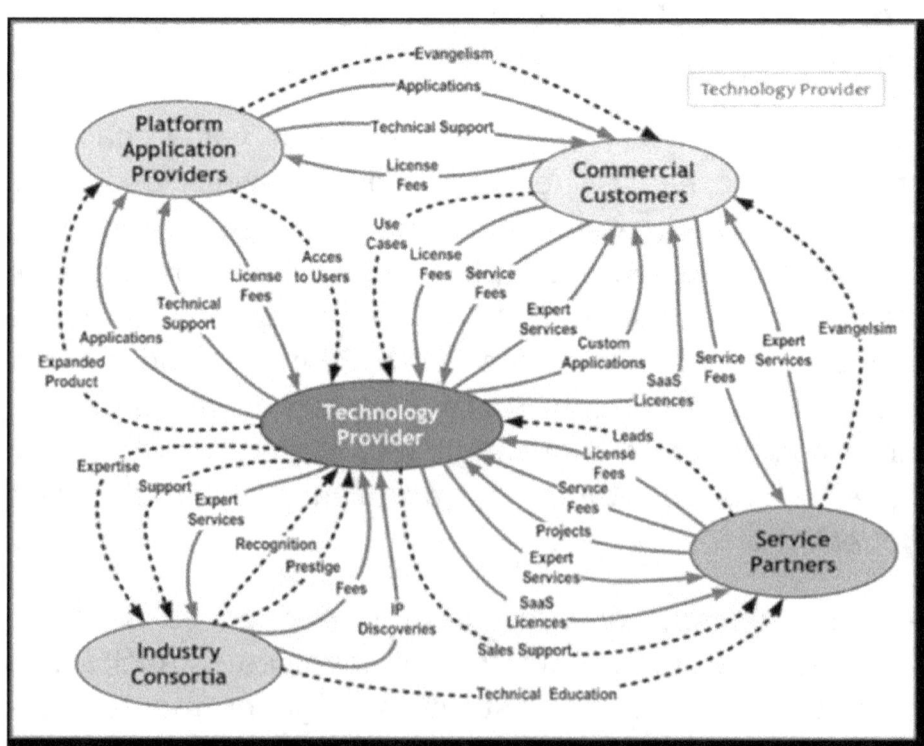

Figure 26, Value Network, Technology Provider

From all the above flows, the thing that has changed lately with sensors and other network technologies like IoT is the Data >> Information, and finally, the upcoming insights flow revolution. Data is becoming an asset for value creation, not only because of the growing amount and quality that is available from many sources, but also because digital data, unlike traditional market research data, is increasingly accurate and real-time. This gives you greater speed and accuracy in understanding your target customers and adapting and controlling your business world. Having better data allows for better decision making for all relevant processes of any business creation. But it is not only better data, but also more data.

More data enables *better analytics* >> *better analytics* enable *better products* >> *better products* enable >> *more customers* which finally enables *more data* and reinforces the loop.

This data revolution supported from Xponentially growing technologies gives birth to innovative *Digital Business Models.* See below a few examples that could not be possible without new technologies (e.g. GPS based location, new sensors, cloud computing, data analytics, AI, wireless and mobile communications) and data insights:

- *Improve own products or services with conversion of data to Insights.* Preventative maintenance of high value products (airplane motors) or improve manufacturing processes or preventative healthcare with fitness sensors and real-time data insights.

- *Subscription model.* Monthly payments for access to services, e.g. Netflix for TV, and software applications sold as SaaS (Software as a Service, monthly subscription payments) e.g. Salesforce.

- *Combine data with products to increase quality and value.* When TomTom started collaborating with telecom operators, the user data not only allowed more map improvement, but also provided better insight into road usage to plan better routes.

- *Access instead of ownership.* Access to a room for one or more nights (AirBnB) or a car for one hour (Zipcar).

- *Ecosystem model.* A lot of independent products that when used together, have much higher value, e.g. the Google and Apple ecosystem.

- *Providing services based on data (DaaS)*
   - UBER uses the demand information to plan shared rides.
   - UBEREATS provides value to their suppliers by informing them when their quality is deteriorating.

- *Shared transportation.* Think about all transporttation services like UBER, DiDi, MOBIKE and other similar services.

- *Expanding to other industries.* See examples below with Google and Amazon.

How to design digital business models

1. *Design the Value Network/ecosystem* (e.g. customers, partners, NGOs, government) with all ecosystem participants and the various flows and relationships among them.

2. *Identify your position/role in the ecosystem.*

3. *Use data to solve problems or address needs* and develop new value proposition options, including payments, by using data or derived data.

4. *Create a roadmap of how the value proposition and business model* will develop over time, taking into account the available or derived data, partnerships, technology roadmaps, channel developments and other relevant ecosystem and business model attributes.

5. *Use the secret of the digital business models:* As many of the new Xponentially growing technologies (cloud computing, machine learning, AI) go across industries, use the existing technologies you have to transfer/create value to a new industry and capture value for your core business, as we have seen in Chapter 1 and repeated here, as it is essential to be understood.

Google: Google is using various technologies (Mobile AI, Cloud Computing Machine Learning/AI, High Speed Internet, IoT, Biotechnology and Genetics and Crowd Sourcing) that cross many industries (Entertainment, Communication, Education, Finance, Transportation, Military, Medical) to expand their activities beyond their main revenue generator (Search/Google Ads). Google or Alphabet creates value with Google Play (media), Android (handsets) and Google Wallet (retail), and captures value through ad sales (advertising)—its core business.

Amazon: Creates value with Kindle (handset) and Amazon apps (media) and captures value through e-commerce, its core business.

3.8 Summary and deliverables

In this chapter, we have explored the process to find options for growth by eliminating pain points across the customer experience cycle, finding new potential customer groups and deciding which new value propositions to target to which customer group. We talked about the changing innovation principles of the 21st Century and we introduced the **Xponential culture matrix** to support the creation of new ideas and concepts. Finally, we described the process to create new options of growth by following eight different pathways.

By the end of this process, there are two major deliverables for each of the eight pathways or subset or combination of pathways chosen to be analysed:

1. Make a list of the important findings/insights and factors of competition per pathway, or a new business model including new factors of competition.

2. First, make a description of which factors of competition need to be:

- Eliminated
- Decreased
- Increased
- Created

Conclusion

Although there are many lessons to be learned from this chapter, the most important are:

- **We can always create opportunities to expand the market by eliminating customer pain points or blocks.**

- **To grow faster, you need a growth mindset and to follow the relevant innovation principles.**

- **Ensure that people discover and experience themselves the need for change as well as talking directly to customers and other ecosystem stakeholders.**

- **Many exponentially growing technologies are crossing industries, and by enabling value creation in other industries, you can recapture the value in your own core business.**

- **New digital business models are enabling Xponential growth.**

Chapter 4: Create Xponential growth strategy per pathway

As figure 27 shows, the 4th step is about creating an Xponential growth strategy per pathway, which is about making choices. It is deciding which factors of competition to **eliminate, reduce, increase** or **create** per pathway and setting the foundation to decide which pathway or pathways and other ideas or combinations of pathways to use.

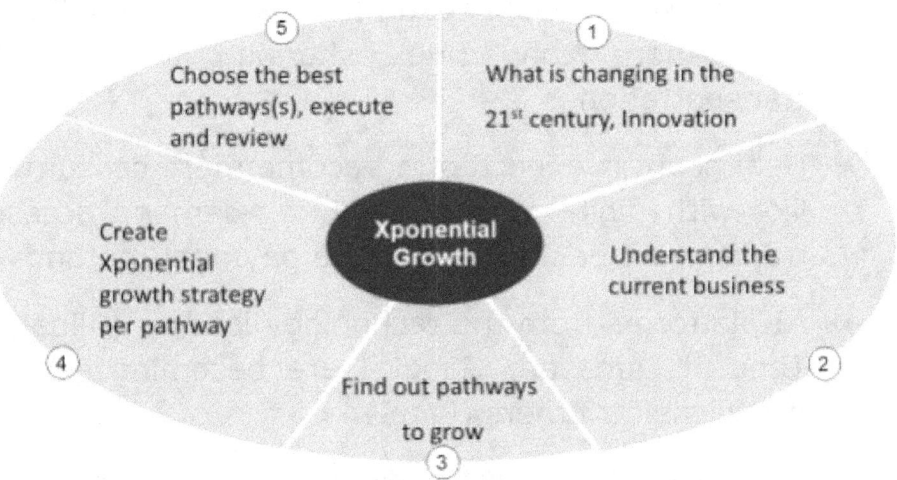

Figure 27

Before you proceed with choices per pathway, you need to devote some time on what the recent major trends from the technology industries are, as a source of additional information and inspiration before you create the Xponential strategy:

- Technology companies in the USA recently became the biggest investors in R&D in relation to any other industry above 15% of sales. Amazon leads the pack with almost $25 billion USD investment in R&D per year, followed by Google. Other countries, and especially China, are following fast.

- Video is growing fast as an enabler of online and retail purchases.

- There is a gradual shift from *buying* to *subscribing*, as many business models are changing: e.g. selling software to selling SaaS (Capex to Opex) in examples such as Netflix, Amazon Prime, Spotify, Dropbox, Sony Playstation Plus and Stitch Fix.

- In the west, people spend less on owning vehicles and more on ride sharing and public transportation.

- Healthcare is expected to become more consumer-like with digital engagement, on-demand access, transparent pricing and simple payment methods.

- AI platforms from the technology leaders (Alibaba, Tencent, Amazon, Google) are becoming service platforms for others (PaaS).

- Cybersecurity, malware volume is growing exponenttially with more than 10X increase the last two years.

- Voice recognition becomes more accurate and grows fast, aspiring to become the dominant way of interaction with everyday devices and systems.

- The New Era is about: AI, Blockchain and IoT

As AI, Blockchain and IoT will be significant contributors to the major changes ahead of us we analyse these three technologies more extensively. In the last 50 years, the technology world has experienced tremendous growth, with various technological revolutions like: Semiconductors, PC, Internet, Mobile, Search, Cloud, 3D Printing, and Biotechnology, to name a few. In most cases the fundamental research has been funded from governments, e.g. Internet from DARPA, and to a lesser extend from large companies. After the research stage, companies used the research outcomes and developed products to test the market.

Especially for the case of the Internet, it has undergone three phases so far and it is entering the 4th.

The 1st phase was about research in DARPA (Defense research agency in USA), with the creation of a limited but safe network with few participants for almost two decades (1960s to 1980s). The 2nd phase, mainly in the 90s, has been characterized from development of open protocols superimposed on the solid communication layer of the Internet, enabling basic services, and especially browsers, that created exponential growth of various applications and platforms in the 3rd phase. The 2nd phase is about decentralization, and all companies that built applications using the original open protocols assumed that the rules of the game based on the open protocols would not change. Indeed, this happened and the rules of the game changed only in the 3rd phase. The 2nd phase has been characterized from many companies participating and innovating in a level playing field.

The 3rd phase, after 2000 until today, is about tremendous growth of the Internet, characterized from the creation of new and more powerful applications (e.g. mobile applications, cloud computing, video applications, multi-side platforms, to name a few) that gave rise to new, not open protocols created from huge nowadays companies like Google, Apple, Amazon and Facebook. The main difference in the 3rd phase is that these companies have created centralized and partly closed ecosystems reflecting the new era of powerful centralized platforms, creating almost monopolies or oligopolies in their focused areas, dominating the market and collecting the majority of the profits. The centralization of power has disabled partly innovation as the dominant players with deep pockets not only acquire innovative start-ups in early stages but also disable in general start-ups to compete in the Internet space. This is applicable especially in USA as well as in China with Alibaba, Tencent and Baidu.

In the 3rd phase of the Internet the dominant technologies were **Mobile, Social** and **Cloud Computing.** Using the **Gartner** emerging technologies hype cycle, let's evaluate the evolution of Cloud computing from 2010 to 2017. (See Figure 28 on the following page, shown vertically for clarity). In 2010, Cloud Computing had just topped the Peak of Inflated Expectations and private cloud computing was still rising. Cloud/Web platforms were also shown, along with mobile application stores, to acknowledge the growing interest in platforms for application development and delivery.

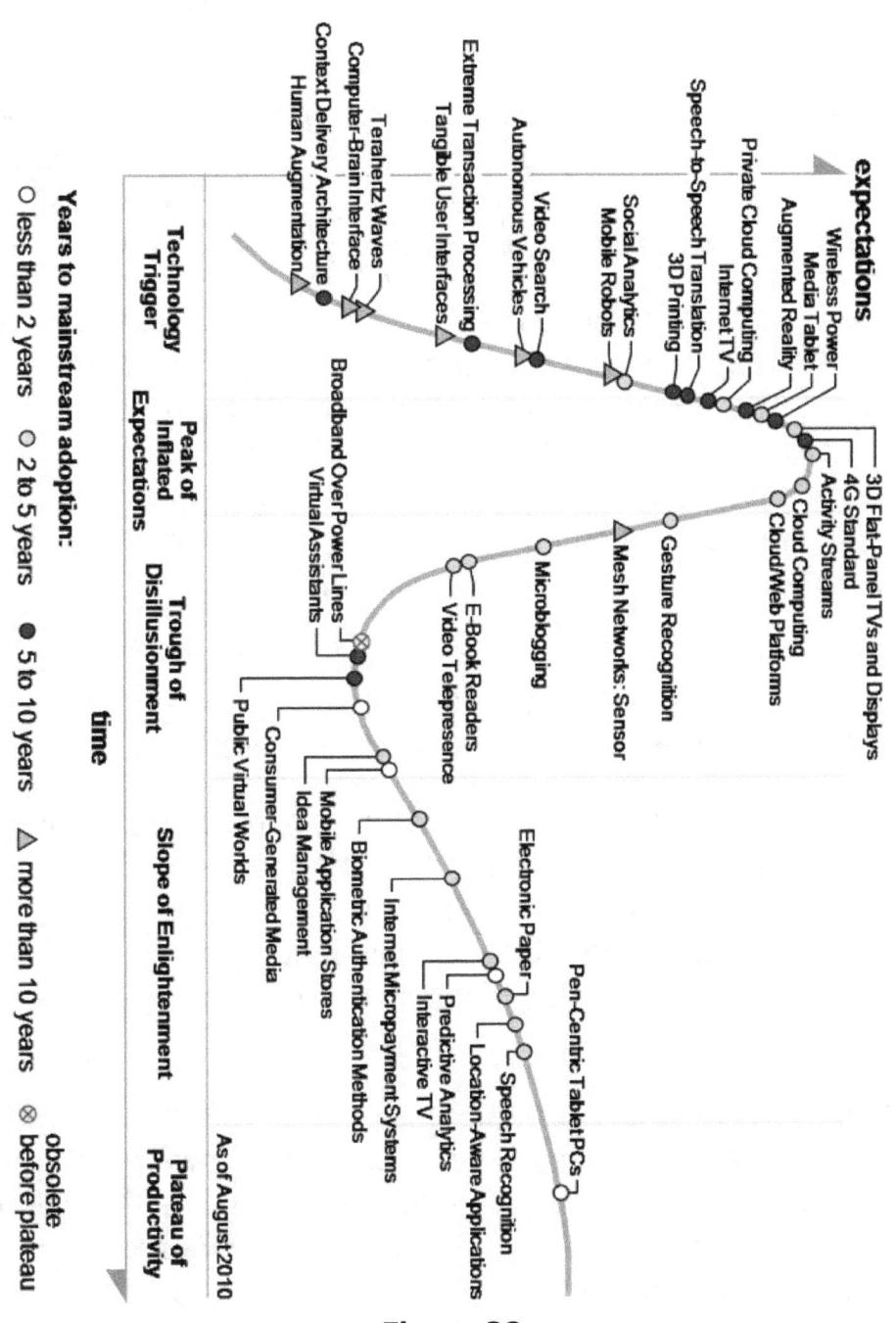

Figure 28

In 2017/2018, Cloud computing is almost mainstream, being in the late stages of the plateau of productivity, and has moved out of the **Gartner** hype cycle of emerging technologies.

Moving to 2018, we can see below that the new hot technologies at the Peak of Inflated Expectations stage (See Gartner hype cycle 2017) are **Blockchain, AI/Machine learning/Deep learning** and **IoT**.

While simpler nowadays and specific area applications of AI (BOTS, Voice recognition, Image recognition, Automated voice response, Digital marketing) and **IoT** are growing and will be widespread the coming two to five years, **Blockchain** applications will take more than five years to become widespread and general AI will take more than ten years to mature.

Before we talk about the 4th Internet phase, which is just starting, let's devote a few words on the importance of **AI/Machine learning, Blockchain** and **IoT**.

AI and machine learning has the potential to benefit almost all industries, from supply chain to drug research. It will be a must-use technology, as it will be soon become impossible for conventional engineering solutions to handle the increasing amounts of available data.

With IoT and 5G digital, businesses will move away from siloed business ventures and toward inter-connected ecosystems. (See Figure 29 on the following page, shown vertically for clarity.) Businesses must think about how to create platform-based business models and what technology is needed to support that move.

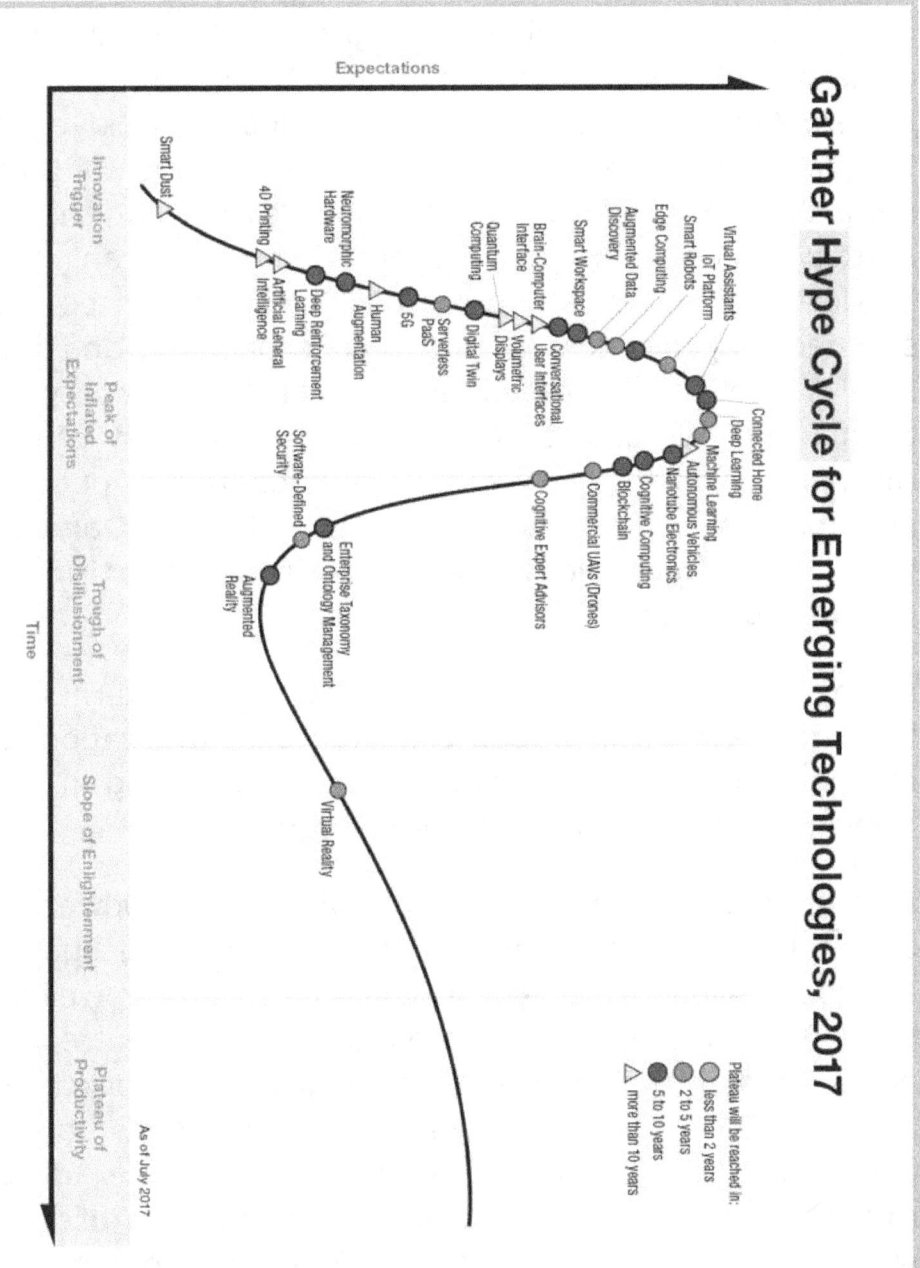

Figure 29

Finally, **Blockchain** applications might seem like they are just around the corner. While there are siloed pilot projects using Blockchain even in China where cryptocurrencies are banned (e.g. agricultural productivity applications), most initiatives are still in the foundational stages. **Ethereum** is finalizing the foundational layer of the platform, and according to their founders it will take more than five years until the higher layers that enable interoperability with other platforms creating meaningful applications for users will be available. Enterprises are still deciding how to navigate this technology, and the lack of proven use cases, as well as the volatility of bitcoin, have created concerns about the viability of the technology while they have pilot projects to find out the potential of the technology. Long-term, **Gartner** believes this technology will lead to **a reformation of whole industries.**

As the transition from the 2nd phase of the Internet to the 3rd has been characterized from decentralization to centralization, what will happen, or is happening in the transition from the 3rd to the 4th stage?

As we described above the centralization of power to only a few players (Apple, Google, Amazon, Facebook, Microsoft, Alibaba, Tencent, Uber, Didi, Baidu) as well as the 2008/2009 financial recession inspired entrepreneurs to start using new technologies like Blockchain and create crypto-networks. These networks allow decentralization based on **open source code, data privacy/security, competition for better results,** as well as **fair economic incentives** to developers and other network participants in the form of tokens. This trend has started in 2009 with the Bitcoin network and has been intensified since 2015 with Ethereum and many other crypto-networks and crypto-currencies.

While AI has been adopted and will be dominated from the existing players like Google, Amazon, FB, Apple and others, new start-ups are focusing on IoT platforms and Blockchain based crypto-networks that support not only decentralization but ensure that all network participants are rewarded, even if they exit the network after contribution.

While AI will support the existing centralization, IoT and Blockchain will be the cornerstones of the 4th phase of the Internet with powerful decentralized platforms and much better economic incentives for all participants. At the same time AI will also support the creation of the powerful decentralized platforms by solving challenging problems like:

- **Scalable Blockchain databases**
- **Decentralized cloud computing**
- **Decentralized data protocols**
- **Decentralized privacy and security technologies**

Concluding, the coming 10-15 years of the Internet will be a mix of centralized and decentralized networks where the existing dominant players are focusing on centralized networks while new players are emerging with decentralized networks and platforms challenging the status quo and creating a level playing field for many more market participants similar to the 2nd phase of the Internet.

Finally, we conclude this part with two statements from two influential people:

"AI is one of the most important things humanity is working on and it is more profound than electricity or fire...AI is really important, but we have to be concerned about it." Sundar Pichai, CEO of Google, 2/2018

"The Internet, Big Data, Artificial Intelligence and The Real Economy should be interconnected." Xi Jingping, President of China - Xinhua State News Agency, 12/9/17

Now we continue with the process steps we need to follow to create the Xponential growth strategy per pathway.

4.1 Analyze comments, extract insights and align in the team per pathway

In this stage, by analysing the findings in more detail, first individually and then in a team, you ensure that you can enrich your insights, as repetition is the mother of learning and sets the foundation to make better decisions as to which factors to **eliminate, reduce, increase** or **create** in order to create Xponential growth. Additionally, if one team is responsible for more than one pathway, the cross learning can help to make better decisions, and that is another reason why the finalisation of the new factors of competition is done in Step 4 and not in Step 3.

4.2 Decide which factors of competition to eliminate, reduce, increase or create per pathway

In this part of the process, you decide which factors to eliminate, reduce, increase or create by asking the following questions. These questions are similar to what we ask when we want to create a new business model (see Chapter 3):

- Which of the factors that the industry takes for granted should be eliminated?
- Which factors should be reduced well below the industry's standard?
- Which factors should be increased well above the industry's standard?
- Which factors that the industry has never offered should be created?

What is essential is to focus on concrete factors as well as on both differentiation/new value creation and cost reduction.

To make all choices made easily understandable you use the *Winning Formula*, shown in Figure 30 on the following page. The winning formula lists the decisions per pathway of which factors of competition will be **eliminated, decreased, increased** and **newly created**. It is essential to mention that the most difficult is to eliminate factors of competition or create new ones. At the same time, eliminating and creating new factors of competition enables the biggest growth and profitability. Only with increases or decreases of factors of competition, there is no major differentiation in order to create Xponential growth.

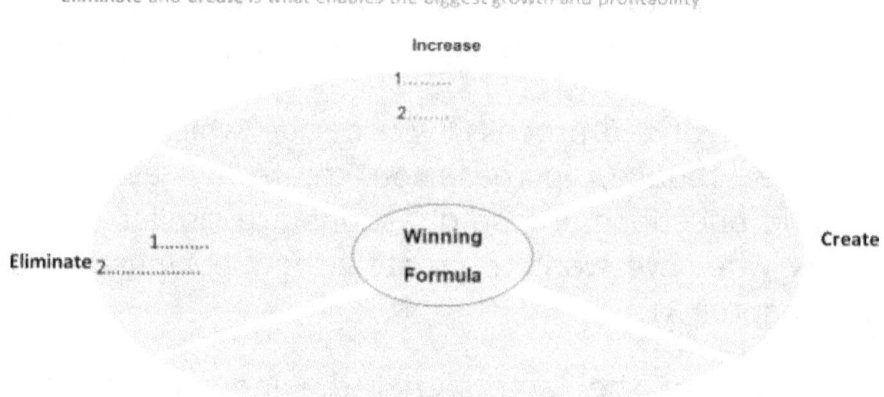

Figure 30, Winning Formula

In the case of **UBER**, see the winning formula in Figure 31, the creation of new value has been enabled from new technologies and conscious choices have been made to reduce costs as well as to enable efficiency and flexibility.

Eliminate: Cash payments and booking by calling.

Decrease: Prices and price stability to allow for higher prices when the demand is high.

Increase: Service orientation and innovation.

Create: Booking by app, payments through mobile/credit card and add more value and create new services by knowing the car and customer's location.

The abovementioned new value creations were new for customers at the time of introduction and have been enabled after 2007/2008 from the newly available and Xponentially growing technologies (mobile tech and crowdsourcing enabled from GPS/navigation technologies).

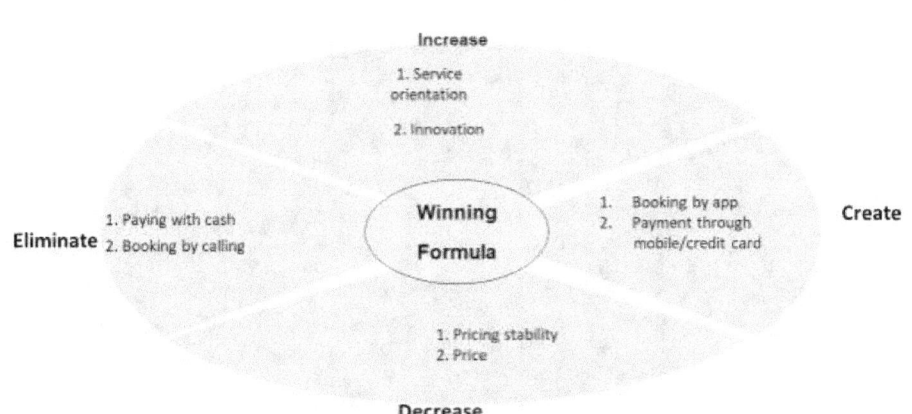

Figure 31, Winning Formula UBER

In the case of **Apple/iPhone** in the period 2008-2009, see the winning formula in Figure 32. The creation of new value has been enabled from new technologies and very conscious choices have been made to reduce costs as well as enable flexibility and to drastically improve the user experience. The main focus was in eliminating factors of competition as well as creating new ones.

Eliminate: Hard keyboard and replace with the touch screen.

Create: Touch screen with a new, better design, and for many, a better user experience, an app store with thousands of apps and great Internet browsing. We all know the exponential growth of Apple over the last 15 years, and the iPhone has contributed to the great majority of this growth. The elimination of the keyboard resulted in cost reduction and the newly created factors of competition have been enabled by new technologies (mobile tech, display technology, cloud computing and apps).

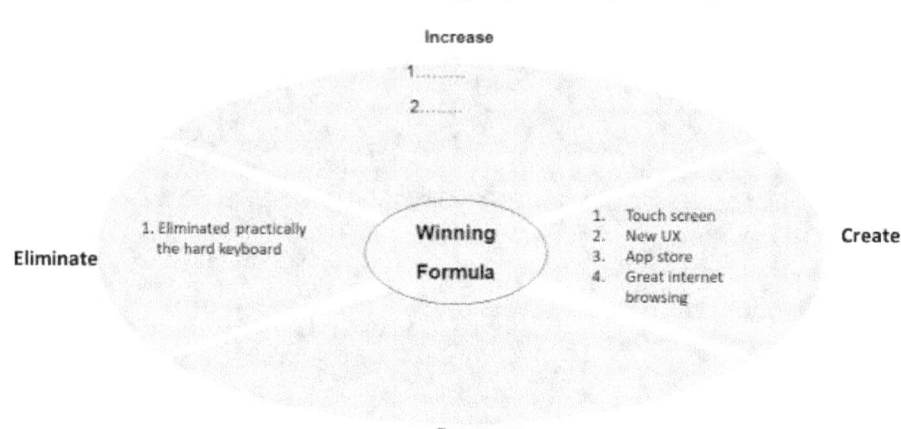

Winning Formula iPhone, Figure 32

Another example is about the cable TV industry, where **Netflix** entered the market and not only created new factors of competition (ability to watch from anywhere and ability to watch full seasons), but also eliminated factors of competition (news, commercials). Netflix made use of new technologies (video streaming) as well as IP technology, which helps to expand worldwide with lower operational costs and provides a timely increase in broadband bandwidth and connectivity in general. Nowadays, Netflix is following the growth in Internet connectivity and bandwidth increase to expand almost all over the planet Earth.

For **Netflix**, the winning formula is in Figure 33; the creation of new value has been enabled from new technologies and very conscious choices have been made to eliminate factors of competition and reduce costs as well as enable efficiency and flexibility.

Eliminate: News and commercials. The former reduces costs, while the latter reduces revenues and eliminates complaints about too many commercials.

Decrease: Price and installation complexity decrease cause an increase in demand and reduce customer service costs.

Increase: Ease of installation is reducing customer service costs and the number of devices you can watch increases the demand.

Create: Ability to watch from anywhere as well as watch full seasons help to increase demand.

The Netflix winning formula has created a winning business model, resulting in the highest ROI from all known high technology companies over the last ten years.

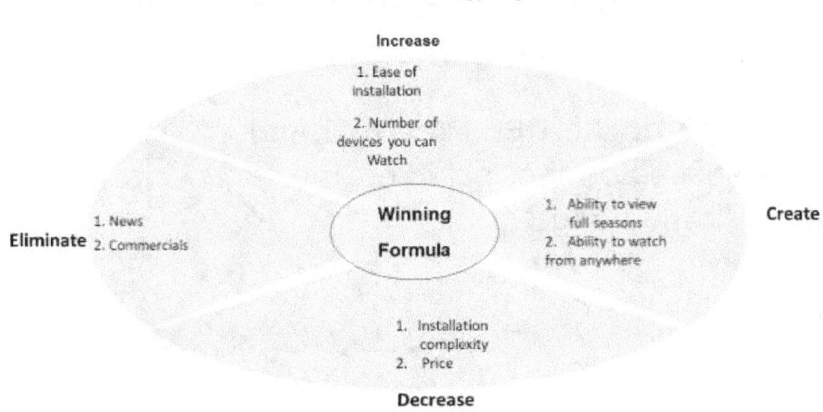

Winning Formula Netflix, Figure 33

4.3 Create the new strategic map for the specific pathway

To create the new strategic map for a pathway, you use the winning formula and then follow the rules:

- *Eliminate*: Factors should score 0 in the new strategic map.
- *Create*: Factors should be high.
- *Price is the first factor*, then follow the *eliminate* factors, then the *decrease*, then the *increase*, and finally, the *create* to avoid having ups and downs across the whole graph.
- *Plot all company factors.*
- *Add the new company tagline*, reflecting the new positioning.
- *Then plot the existing competitors and compare. A tagline is essential to fully reflect the new strategic map/positioning.*
- *High growth strategic maps are normally simple.*
- *A high growth strategic map must be different from competition, must be focused* (it is easily visible where the company differentiates from competition) *and with a compelling tagline.*

For the case of the UBER or DIDI and the taxi industry, see the strategic map including the tagline in Figure 34 on the following page.

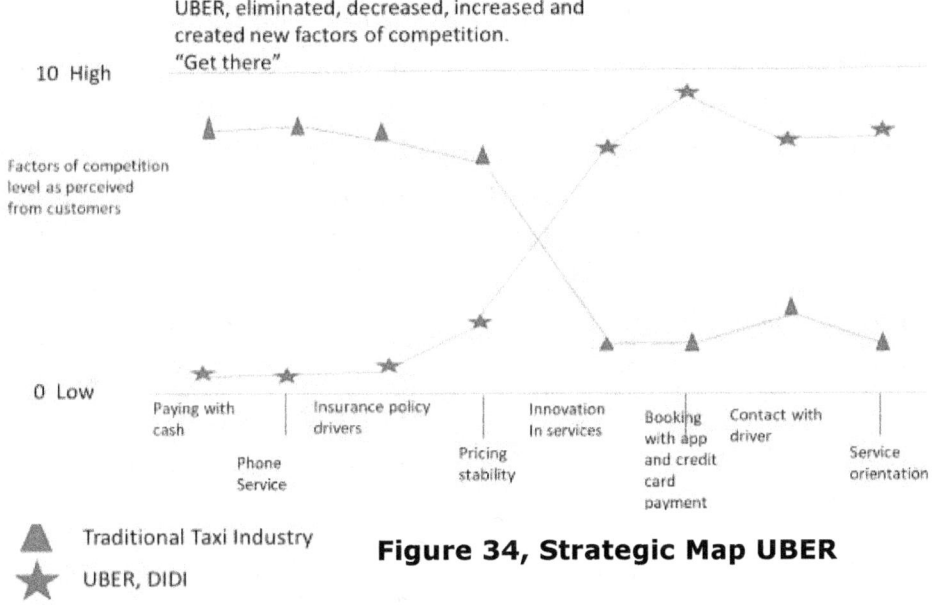

Figure 34, Strategic Map UBER

For the case of iPhone and the mobile phone industry, see the strategic map including the tagline in Figure 35.

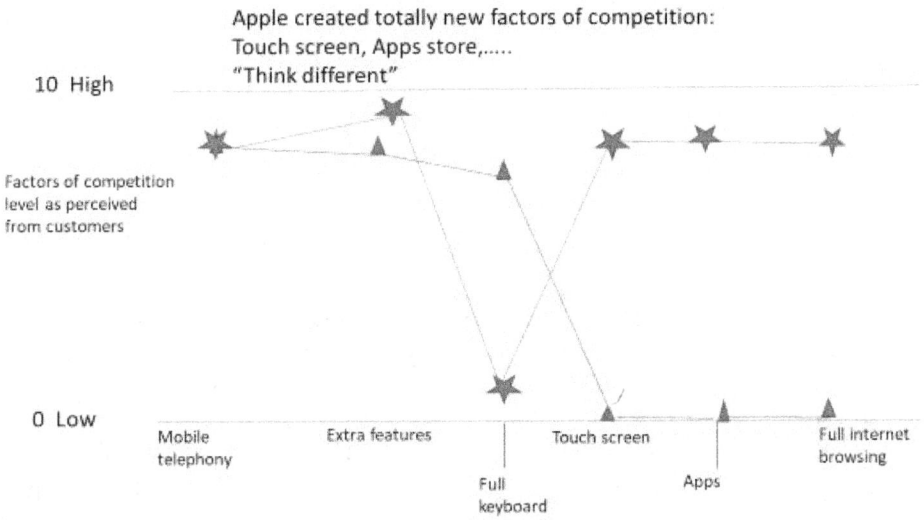

Figure 35, Strategic Map iPhone and Mobile Phone Industry

For Snapchat challenging Facebook, see the strategic map, including the tagline in Figure 36. In this case, it is very clear that there are differences between the two companies, but there are neither major eliminations nor major new value creations. It is more about increases and decreases of existing factors of competition. This fact is reflected in the valuation of Snapchat, which is not as high as its investors might have expected. The key reasons are that there are no eliminations or major new value creations versus the combination of Facebook and Instagram, which are working to imitate the differences.

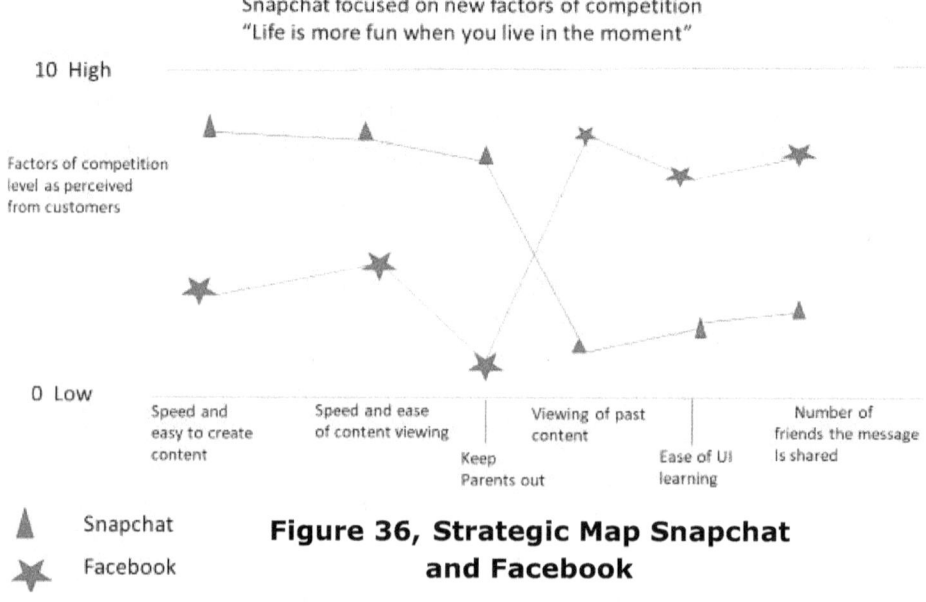

Figure 36, Strategic Map Snapchat and Facebook

For the case of Netflix and the cable industry, see the strategic map including the tagline in Figure 37 on the following page. Netflix has not only created a differentiating value proposition with new strong factors of competition, but has also eliminated factors as well, resulting in strong growth of revenues and company valuation.

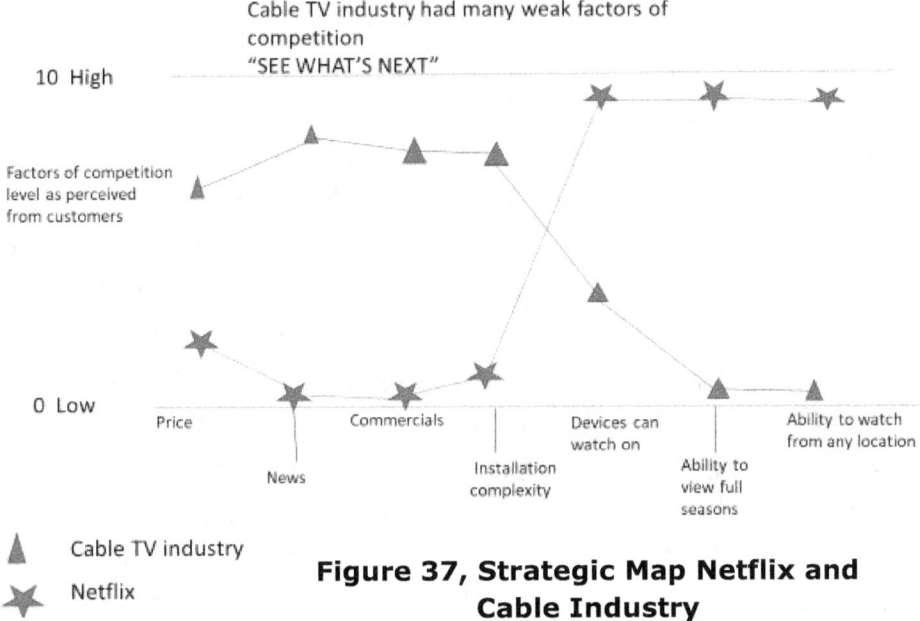

Figure 37, Strategic Map Netflix and Cable Industry

After you have created the strategic map and the winning formula, it is time to focus on the customer benefits and the economic benefits of the pathway.

4.4 Evaluate and explain the economic benefits - repeat for the selected pathways

Using the four categories (eliminate, decrease, increase, create) for all factors of competition, and their cost reductions or additions and new value, evaluate the economic benefits. See Figure 38, which is the list of cost decreases and increases as well as new value/ benefits.

The economic benefits are presented in two parts:
- The company view
- The customer view

After this is done for the specific pathways, the same process needs to be repeated for all the selected pathways of potential growth. In the case of the economic model of Netflix, Figure 38 shows clearly what the cost increases and decreases are, as well as new value creations for both the company and the customer. Netflix has decreased price, which has given steady increase in customer growth, resulting in 22% revenue growth, increased ease of installation which gave lower customer service costs, eliminated revenue from commercials, and used IP technology which decreased cost of operations, and finally, created new factors of competition: you can watch Netflix anywhere with an increased number of devices as well as you can watch full seasons.

Company View	Customer view
- Easier installation xx/% less customer service costs - No revenue from commercials - IP technology, easier to expand globally and lower costs of operations by yy/% - Lower prices means service accessible to more customers and faster growth of revenues by zz%	- Lower Price xx USD - No commercials - Flexibility to watch on any device - No News - View full seasons

Figure 38, Economic Model Netflix—quantify the benefits and costs from the point of view of the customer and the company

For the customer, the benefits are: lower price, no commercials, flexibility to watch from anywhere with more devices and be able to watch full seasons.

4.5 Xponential Growth

After the four chapters, this is the right place to justify the Xponential growth title of this book. Xponential growth is the result of the multiplication of a number of factors. When you multiply an Xponentially growing factor with another one that is growing linearly or Xponentially, the result is Xponential growth. In conclusion, let's now describe which of these factors are reinforcing each other to contribute to even accelerating Xponential growth:

- *The mindset of growth and abundance and why it is possible to achieve 10X improvement or more instead of just 10% or 30%.*
- *Information-based businesses (the number is increasing) are growing Xponentially or becoming Xponentially more efficient.*
- *Many Xponentially growing technologies are crossing industries, and by enabling value creation in other industries, can recapture the value in their own core businesses.*
- *Expansion of the market with new customers.*
- *New digital business models enabling Xponential growth.*
- *Other industry-specific growth factors.*

All or some of the mentioned factors/enablers can be used in the same business, reinforcing each other or multiplying with each other, and as such, creating Xponential growth. Depending on the business, some will be more or less applicable and there will be other more specific growth factors to contribute to further growth. The examples of Google and Amazon mentioned before explained the concept better.

In this part, I will describe a personal experience from a real life example of transformation and exponential growth from a few years ago. For obvious reasons no names or locations will be mentioned.

Company description: Start-up in growth stage; eight years in B to B business; offices in many countries around the world; selling in approximately fifteen countries through partners, and company present almost across the whole value chain from product planning, design, manufacturing (outsourced), marketing and sales with partners.

- Industry: Technology
- People competencies and skills not up to the level for a fast growth and global company ambition.
- Lack of adequate processes for a full value chain and multinational footprint.
- Product/system/quality issues
- Lack of product strategy, product management, innovation processes and outsource processes
- Slow design process
- Slow manufacturing and supply partners
- With a few exceptions low quality sales partners
- Good brand name in a few countries and won a few key projects. Something to build upon.

- Struggling with profitability and growth as many companies in this stage of development
- Execution of projects: Not mature with delays and quality issues
- Relatively okay from cash point of view. One problem less among so many.

Phase I

- After one month talking to all key people and attempting to understand the Value Chain, I started with Marketing and Sales.
- As all companies are succeeding or failing due to people, decided in parallel to focus on people changes starting from the 2nd month, when I hired a few experienced people and together with the very few existing competent people started redesigning the processes and planning replacements. Together with the experienced professionals, we made a plan to change 60 % of the people (within 6-9 months) in the headquarters without yet touching the marketing and sales subsidiaries worldwide.
- With the better-qualified people we brought on board, many of the existing employees decided themselves to leave, making life partly easier for both themselves and the company.
- Evaluated all short-term expenses that could be reduced and took the necessary actions.
- After 90 days the first big surprise. We started negotiations with a fortune 500 company, and

within a few months we reached a basic agreement of preliminary terms for a joint venture to be followed within months from a due diligence before we go to the negotiation details, including the lengthy legal process.

- Eight months later and preparing for the due diligence process, we had replaced 60% of the people and had redesigned all processes.

- Nine months later a successful due diligence process took place, when we were complimented about a few processes that had been considered world class and many good people!

- At the same time, and in order to increase the value of the company before final negotiation started, we acquired a technology start up partner, a company crucial for us to create competitive solutions. This had been discussed a few months earlier and executed within a few months.

- As all above was going on, we had to improve our product quality, make our offerings more flexible, increase speed of design and execution, address delivery reliability, and finally, sales growth and profitability improvement. To achieve that beyond focus on internal process improvements, we decided to improve the quality of our supply and demand partners. Three new and more competent manufacturing and component suppliers were chosen, and we started evaluating a few new downstream solution sales partners with better capabilities. We also pursued partnership with two

other partners so we could create new innovative solutions together.
- The last three months of the first year on the job have been devoted to the execution of all improvements and joint venture negotiations, which were very lengthy, but at the end we signed the JV agreement twelve months after I came on board.

Phase II

- Our business plan had above **80 % sales growth per year for three years, with two years almost doubling sales.**
- Started by establishing a new Mission/ Transformative purpose, Vision and Operating strategy for the new JV, which we deployed worldwide.
- With more competent and experienced people, better processes, new customer creation and interaction process, better products and systems in the pipeline, better suppliers and better downstream partners, we were optimistic to achieve this challenging growth.
- To find out more about our customers and what to improve we started a detailed NPS (net promoter score) process including many qualitative questions.
- To strengthen our brand in a competitive way we decided to devote more attention to marketing with focus on website, superb marketing content

and materials, PR, partner events and **digital social networking to create a community!**

In general, we positioned the brand with more emotional attributes within a functional industry.

The main challenges we had to eliminate and/or solve were:

1. Avoid to be slowed down being in JV with a big company and we negotiated in advance as much **autonomy** as possible.

2. Life cycle of the most of our projects/solutions were average two years and we needed to grow sales with above 80 % within one year. We managed to achieve it with a list of strategies and tactics:

    i. Attempted to leverage the JV partner for short term sales: It did not work, as we had a completely different business model than the partner who did not have access to our market segments.

    ii. **Changed our business model with a different distribution strategy** to enable shorter term sales: that worked only partly.

    iii. With the newly introduced design processes + new more **flexible systems** + new supply partners we could **speed up** our systems design and delivery by six months as well as offer a lot of flexibility to satisfy many more customer requirements. Consequently, we focused to find and win faster projects (one-year lifecycle) and this strategy worked better.

  iv. With the better people that came on board, as well as more flexible systems and faster deliveries, we started to win projects from competitors as we could deliver faster and better **systems and solutions!**

  v. Some of the better, newly acquired sales partners, also helped to increase sales faster.

3. As we became more competitive **(faster AND better quality AND more flexible AND better partners that build a better ecosystem,...)** we set the foundation for structural growth and we reached agreement with the JV board to invest in more sales resources, so we started hiring people in ten additional attractive locations worldwide.

The first two years after the JV establishment we managed to double our sales and achieved more than 80 % overall growth in sales per year.

What WE learned from this Team Effort:

– Assembling a core team with the best people available for the task is number one priority. Such a drastic, complex and fast turnaround and then excellent growth can only be achieved with a good team of top professionals having the right experiences. Preferably from a different industry, are determined to succeed, are able to think out of the box and are led from an inspiring and disciplined leader.

- To achieve breakthrough, the team needs to have **the right mindset, namely believing that the fast growth is possible;** you need to change multiple business attributes. In this case we focused on: **Flexibility AND Speed AND Better partners AND Better People AND New Customer interaction process AND....**

– JV Partners with different business models and market segments can rarely add value to each other on short to medium term.

– A JV needs **autonomy** to deliver. Innovation cannot be done within an established company which protects the established core business model.

– **Software and systems/solution thinking/acting becomes more and more important in our networked world.**

– Learning by establishing fast feedback loops from market to the company is vital for success.

– Leadership to inspire and focus people behind a bigger and **transformative mission/purpose** than themselves is key.

– **Embracing more and more digital marketing, crowd sourcing and all the new exponential technologies that go across many industries is vital for success.**

4.6 Summary and deliverables

In this chapter, we created the Xponential growth strategy per pathway that consists of the new strategic map with the appropriate tagline, the winning formula, the customer and company benefits, and finally, the economic model. We used four examples and additionally, we explained that logic behind the book name Xponential Growth.

The deliverables of the Xponential growth strategy per pathway are the winning formula, the strategic map, the benefits and economic benefits for both the customer and the company separately. Although the customer benefits and the economic model are both shown in one graph for reasons of space efficiency, they should be drawn separately. The economic model has more financial details than the customer benefits.

Conclusion

- ***What is essential for great results is to focus on concrete factors as well as on both differentiation/new value creation and cost reduction.***
- ***Xponential growth is the result of multiplication of a number of factors, which include both linear and exponential factors.***

Chapter 5: Choose the best pathway(s), execute and review

As Figure 39 shows, the 5th step in your Xponential growth journey is to choose the best pathway(s), execute and review to improve.

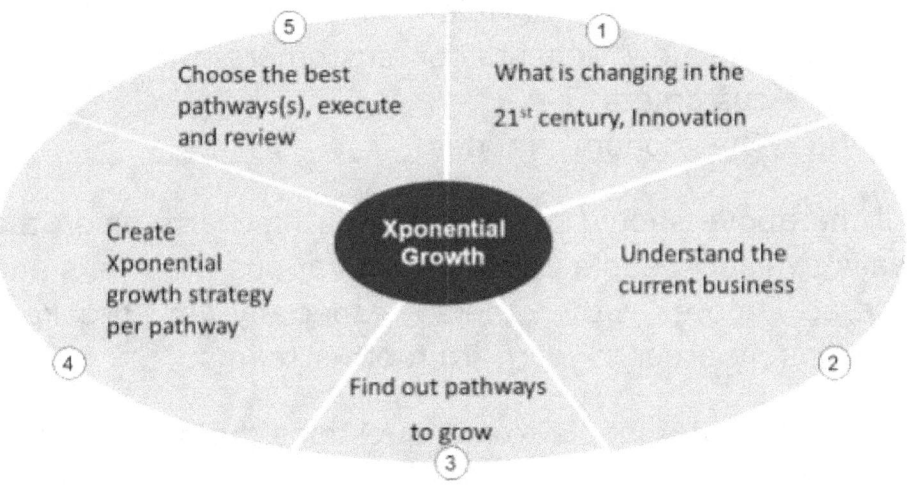

Figure 39

5.1 Evaluation process and management decision

In order to decide what is the best pathway or combination of pathways, or a pathway with only elements from other pathways to choose, you can use the following process:

1. Organise a meeting with all team members who worked in the various pathways and the management team of the company. This meeting is vital for the company's future and it has to be treated accordingly.
2. Present the current business strategic map and business state-of-the-art to remind everyone where the company stands within the current industry.
3. Then ask every team to present their pathway.

   - The new strategic map
   - The winning formula
   - The new benefits for customers and potential customers
   - The economic model

All the above should be available on flipcharts or on the walls to allow people to study the various pathways and interact more with others, especially in breakout sessions, in order to learn from other teams.

4. Stimulate people to ask questions during presentations.
5. Repeat the same for all pathways.
6. Ask people to walk around and study once more the various pathways.
7. Proceed with individual voting on the various pathways.
8. After voting, ask people why they voted for a particular pathway in order to ensure better understanding of the reasons.
9. Ask people what pathways or elements of pathways they would combine and why.

This is the stage when many people realise how creative or innovative the organisation/company in concern can be. The news spreads across the whole organisation and this creates a lot of positive momentum. After the mentioned process is finalised, it is the turn of the management team to work and decide the best way forward. To achieve that, it is suggested to take into account the results of the voting process, answer a few more questions and evaluate if combining pathways offers faster and/or a more robust way to Xponential growth. Applicable questions are:

- Does the new pathway deliver enough value and cost reduction?
- Is the value proposition differentiating enough?
- Can we find ways to increase more value and reduce further cost?
- Is there anything missing or that needs to be modified?
- Can we create more value and reduce costs by combining various pathways or elements of pathways?
- Can we execute?
- What do we need to execute?

In the case of a start-up in the scaling stage, the process will be similar, while the same people that work on the pain points elimination, Xponential culture matrix and/or pathways development are also the decision makers.

In this stage, the experience of the management team of the start-up, or the established company, is very crucial, and practical criteria for the final choice are essential for success. The criteria suggested to be used are the following:

1. **Creates tangible value for potential customers**

   Apple has a seamless experience across expanding family of devices and services; Netflix can be watched anywhere; UBER/DIDI has mobile access, convenience and payments.

2. **Delivers tangible cost decrease**

   Netflix's use of IP technology reduces operating costs by being usable anywhere.

3. **Creates value for the Company**

   Apple controls the operating system and there are advantages to buying all devices from Apple because of interoperability.

4. **It is differentiating enough to create a new strong market positioning**

5. **Receives management support among functions**

6. **Availability of resources (internal or external) to execute**

After a choice is made that can be one pathway enriched with elements from other pathways, or a combination of pathways, it is time to communicate the decision to the whole company.

5.2 Communicate the decision internally and go for a quick market research test

The next step is to communicate the final decision. In case the management team has decided to pursue the extended team choice as a preferred pathway, the decision is very easy to be communicated. In case the management team decided to choose for another pathway or a combination of pathways, the management team needs to organise a new meeting and explain the reasons of the decision. After the decision has been communicated, using a simple prototype of the solution, the team conducts new tests with real customers to receive their final comments, fine-tune the solution and assess the final market potential.

In this stage, there cannot be any major surprises, as the teams have talked to customers or observed customers earlier in the process. At the same time, as this is going to be the major focus and investment of the company going forward, market tests are vital and necessary. The approach of intensive customer involvement, as well as bottom-up and top-down interaction within the company, is essential for creativity, innovation, team spirit, better solutions, faster decisions and finally, successful results.

5.3 Setup an execution team, start implementation and review results

As strategy and execution is more effective to be done from the same team that created the pathway or the pathways, the next step is for management to set up an implementation team consisting of the original team or teams in case of combination of pathways and additional operational people to support the implementation/execution. The task of the team is to take the outputs of Step 4 (strategic map, winning formula, customer and potential customer benefits and economic model) and analyse in more detail the various elements. Setting up a target profit margin and using the target price set, the target cost is the result.

As successful pathways deliver newly created value as well as elimination and decrease of cost elements, achieving the cost target cannot be compromised. Reducing cost is essential and it is not as difficult as people think. As industries are becoming mainstream or commoditising, many factors of competition that are taken for granted offer no value to customers, or to many customers, and consequently, if eliminated or decreased, offer tremendous opportunities for cost reduction. E.g. in the case of Apple/iPhone, the keyboard, and for the case of Netflix, the elimination of news as well as the easier installation and the usage of IP technology has dramatically reduced service and operational costs respectively.

If we take the example of Netflix and the cable industry, we see that Netflix has *created* new value (ability to watch from anywhere as well as watch full seasons), *increased* (ease of installation and number of devices you can watch), *decreased* (price and installation complexity) and *eliminated* (news and commercials). The elimination of news has reduced costs and the elimination of commercials has eliminated complaints about too many commercials, further differentiating Netflix from the competition. It is essential to be understood that the combination of new value creation and cost reduction is vital to create a new successful, high growth and profitable business. It is not OR, but AND.

It is the combination of new value creation AND cost reduction that will achieve great results.

To achieve cost reduction, you need to ask the right questions and be open-minded. See below a few ways that help to achieve cost reduction:

1. *Outsourcing/freelancers.* Look beyond your own resources, focus on your key differentiators, find partners to enable activities that are essential to your operations and are better than you to execute these activities. E.g. Apple/iPhone decided to outsource manufacturing to a more competent partner in China; Uber decided to use freelancers for its drivers, some hotels decided to insource their desserts and snacks. You can crowdsource almost all organisational capabilities in a very competitive performance/cost ratio:

- Design (website, logo, marketing materials using platforms like, Fiverr, Upwork, 99 designs);
- Concept design ideas from communities (Kickstarter, Indiegogo);
- Collaborative innovation/ideation including Crowd (Spigit);
- Concept Validation (reward crowd funding, e.g. Indiegogo);

- Computational resources (Amazon, Rackspace);
- On-demand workforce (Freelancer);
- Prototypes (Techshop);
- Video Commercials (Tongal);
- Incentive competitions for breakthrough solutions with Data (Kaggle);
- Virtual assistants; and
- Financing (Kickstarter, Indiegogo, Crowdfunder).

Do you need in-house Innovation? Any organisation will adapt to opportunities provided by the collaborative-shared economy. Yet *innovation and marketing* provide key differentiators and value drivers. Some considerations and examples are:

a. In-house: concept design+ scouting + business model design + marketing. Crowdsourced: product design, manufacturing, concept testing.

   Depending on the company strategy (what are your differentiators?), competences and market needs/maturity, the mix of in-house versus crowdsourced will change. E.g. in a more mature market, the company might maintain the control of the marketing and crowdsource all the rest, e.g. accessory companies in consumer electronics industry.

b. In-house: concept design + scouting + business model design + product/service design + marketing.

   Crowdsourced: manufacturing, assets (rooms, cars, go to market partners, product design).

Applications are: Consumer electronic companies, professional lighting solutions, Apple, UBER, AirBnB)

As Xponential growth requires outward looking focus and culture, the number of partnerships with third parties will grow fast. Partnerships need to be selected based on criteria supporting your own company values, strategy, and last but not least, similar mindset for faster growth. For any company to grow faster, you need first to develop the individual mindsets. Individuals need to be educated and trained to embrace the 21st Century realities, develop the right mindset and embrace the company strategy for faster growth.

2. *New technologies* can be used to dramatically reduce not only investments, but also operational costs. E.g. data centres can eliminate capital expenditure and convert them to variable operational expenses; market research expenses can be reduced by testing and even validating new concepts with companies like Kickstarter and Indiegogo and intelligent virtual assistants and better UX design can not only automate the call centres but also reduce the customer service costs. For more inspiration of what is possible a few more examples how new technologies can support major cost reductions are mentioned:

- By using telematics and algorithms the rerouting of fleets of vans or trucks are more efficient, saving billions of USD per year.
- Get experts that don't work for you, maximise flexibility (e.g. Freelancer, Mechanical Turk, Fiverr) and reduce fixed costs.

- Fast prototyping, using specific equipment that otherwise could not be afforded: Prototypes (Techshop or equivalent), many successful devices have been created with Techshop resources in USA, e.g. the Square device (mobile payments).

3. *Motivated employees as well as engaged* ones are essential for success for both cost reductions and new value creations. In Chapter 3 we talked about the people approach in order to create success and here we repeat a few success factors:

- *Involve all team members from the beginning, be open, acknowledge that the task is difficult and that with collaboration you will succeed.*

- *Ensure people discover and experience themselves the need for change as well as talking directly to customers and other ecosystem stakeholders.*

- *Assemble one team that will do both strategy and execution to avoid the "not invented here" syndrome as well as people who are motivated to execute the strategy they developed.*

- *Treat all employees as equally important, as all are important to deliver the company promise. In many successful organisations a few management concepts are common:*
    - Management is there to support employees to deliver their promise
    - Employees are company shareholders
    - Employees have bonuses linked to customer delight
    - Employee training is key to the organisation

Before you start implementation, you need to move your attention to the business model where the team analyses it in more detail. Using the strategic map, the winning formula, the benefits for customers and potential customers and the economic model, we can now create the overall business model using, e.g., the business model canvas tool.

In case the final solution is a combination of more than one pathway and/or elements of pathways, a new set of strategic maps, winning formula, customer and potential customers' benefits as well as the economic model need first to be made before we create the overall business model. See Chapter 3 for more details.

Implementing the final strategy, it is advised to start small, execute, review, improve and then expand to grow bigger. This gradual implementation approach is essential for success, as the opposite can be risky with high investment in case major changes need to happen after review. Well-known examples of such gradual and successful implementations are the Apple stores, where Apple started with two stores and then expanded gradually; Facebook started in one university, expanded to ten universities, then a few states and then nationwide before it went global. A similar approach has been followed from Netflix.

Ending this chapter, we consider it vital to mention that living in Xponential times in order to remain competitive and grow faster, it is necessary to be competent with new Xponentially growing technological innovations, namely AI, IoT, VR/AR, data analytics, cybersecurity, etc. Education and training of people with various applications of technologies as well embracing the right mindset as has been discussed are essential factors for success.

5.4 Summary and deliverables

In this chapter, we have explained the process of choosing and implementing a pathway or combination of pathways in order to accelerate growth. To choose the best pathway(s) we introduced criteria for the management team and explained again the importance of the combination of new value creation AND cost reduction. Finally, we presented a few methods to reduce cost as well as explained the right mindset for individuals and teams needed for success.

The deliverables for this chapter are namely:

- Choice of pathway or combination of pathways;
- Communication and implementation plan for the 1st stage; and
- Review plan and the implementation of the next stage.

Conclusion

- **Great results will be achieved with teamwork where all people involved are fully engaged.**
- **It is the combination of new value creation AND cost reduction that will achieve great results.**
- **Test with customers the final solution, improve, start small, execute, review, improve and then expand to grow bigger.**

Epilogue

Xponential growth is the result of multiplication of a number of factors. In the 20th Century, marketing gurus talked about geometric growth based on multiplying linear factors, like customer growth, average price increase and frequency of purchases. In the 21st Century, we talk about Xponential growth, as we have a combination of Xponentially growing factors as well as linear. Some of these factors are:

- *The mindset of growth and abundance and why it is possible to achieve improvement of 10X or more instead of just 10% or 30%.*
- *Information-based businesses (the number is increasing) are growing Xponentially or becoming Xponentially more efficient.*
- *Many exponentially growing technologies are crossing industries and by enabling value creation in other industries, you can capture back the value in your own core businesses.*
- *Expansion of the market with new customers.*
- *New digital business models enabling Xponential growth.*
- *Other growth factors that are industry dependent.*

Companies that follow the Xponential growth strategy will accelerate their innovation and growth. Companies that will follow 20th Century strategies risk to be disrupted or not being able to be follow the growth of the market leaders and become on medium to long term irrelevant.

Thank you for reading this book. I hope that the Xponential growth journey has been inspirational for you and that you have learned many ideas to apply for your business and more. Wishing you a lot of success in whatever way you define it.

If you enjoyed this book or received value from it in any way, then I'd like to ask you for a favour. Would you be kind enough to leave a review for this book on Amazon? It'd be greatly appreciated! To leave a review please go to https://TenX2.com/book.

To find out more, or if you are interested to apply, please check www.TenX2.com.

Exhibits

Exhibit 1: Xponential Culture Matrix – 25 questions to generate new ideas and concepts

1. How can big scale or big purpose mindset with experimentation using existing technologies/platforms create innovation?

2. How can big scale or big purpose mindset support creation of a better business model?

3. How can big scale or big purpose enable faster adoption?

4. How can big scale or big purpose support AND AND in our Business model (BM)?

5. How can big scale or big purpose support to leverage the crowd, underutilised assets and virtual supply chain?

6. How can autonomy and speed with experimentation create innovation?

7. How can autonomy and speed enable a new BM?

8. How can autonomy and speed enable faster adoption?

9. How can AND AND mindset, autonomy and speed reinforce each other?

10. How can autonomy and speed support to leverage crowd, underutilised assets and the cloud?

11. How can you involve community or crowd in low cost experiments?

12. How can community or crowd enable a new business model?

13. How can you involve better communities or crowd in faster market adoption?

14. Can community or crowd support AND AND in your BM?

15. How can you leverage better the community and crowd?

16. Which technologies and how do they enable to dematerialise or demonetise your business model?

17. Which technologies enable a better or different business model?

18. Which technologies can you embrace that will support faster adoption?

19. Which technologies can support AND AND in your BM and how?

20. Which technologies can support leveraging the crowd, leveraging underutilised assets, enrich the supply chain and how?

21. Which data insights support the discovery of future customer needs?

22. How can better customer or process insights enable a better or different business model? Can you transplant a BM from another industry to your own?

23. Which Insights can enable faster adoption and how?

24. Which Insights support AND AND in your BM?

25. What and how can better insights leverage the crowd and enrich the supply chain?

Exhibit 2: Innovation in the future – Questions

As beyond purpose, capabilities and systems are vital for success, the following questions help you to analyse your current innovation capabilities and systems:

1. To what extend do you engage and interact with your community and crowd (customers, suppliers, partners)? Can you give examples?

2. Are you actively busy to increase the information content in your business? What is information based in your business?

3. To what extend do you use algorithms to improve the speed of decision making and automate more your processes?

4. Do you promote experimentation in your innovation process? What?

5. Do you allow failure and encourage risk taking?

6. Are you thinking big enough?

7. Do you use the right metrics to track Innovation? Are these transparently shared within the organisation?

8. Do you allow for autonomy in your innovation groups? To what extent is decision making decentralised?

9. Do you use advanced social tools for communication, collaboration and knowledge sharing? What?

10. Do you optimise processes through experimenttation?

11. Is your leadership team ready for the challenge?

12. Are you making consistent effort to create the right culture?

13. How are you going to leverage the two billion consumers that will join online the coming five to seven years?

14. How can you retain the talent you need to power a true digital transformation?

15. How can you attract the talent you need to fill the gaps in your skills base?

If you enjoyed this book or received value from it in any way, then I'd like to ask you for a favour. Would you be kind enough to leave a review for this book on Amazon? It'd be greatly appreciated!

About the Author

Mike is an innovation management consultant as well as business and management coach specialising in transformational leadership, innovation, Xponential growth, team breakthroughs and transformations. He has served 3x as CEO of global business units in multinationals (Philips Electronics, Siemens), founded and/or lead three technology start-ups and has three decades of leadership experience with at least 3x fast turnarounds. He worked in both B2C and B2B industries (consumer electronics, digital communications, energy efficiency and digital lighting solutions), has created and led innovative scalable global portfolios and systems, and he is reinventing, simplifying, automating, growing effectively and leveraging the community as well as external assets. He has three university degrees, has lived in six countries in Europe and Asia and now lives in Hong Kong.

https://www.linkedin.com/in/mikemastroyiannis/